This book belongs to

_____

COPYRIGHT NOTICE

Copyright @2023 by Bhavana Rehani

All rights reserved. No part of this publication may be reproduced, stored in a retrieval system, or transmitted in any form or by any means, electronic, mechanical, photocopying, recording, or otherwise without written permission of the publisher.

Note to parents

Dear parents

I'm a mom of two amazing kids. Having tried many early reading books to help them start their journey into reading, I realized that many of these books have long and difficult words. Kids often find such books intimidating since they need a lot of help to read them completely.

Young kids can gain reading confidence early by starting with 2 and 3 letter words, especially in the right order.
In this book, we stick to 1, 2 and 3 letter words only. We start with words that are easier to sound phonetically and those that have the similar ending syllables.

This helps kids add numerous words to their reading vocabulary with minimal effort. Having built this confidence, we then move on to words that are tougher to understand phonetically.

To help them learn these tougher 3 letter words we have numerous practice exercises that mix up easier words with tougher ones. Each practice exercise consists of 15 words.

With regular reading and practice, the littlest of readers should soon be able to read all the words in this book and enjoy the short stories at the end of the book.
So let's get started!

by	
my	

so	
no	
go	

to	
do	

cat

rat

sat

bat

mat

fat

hat

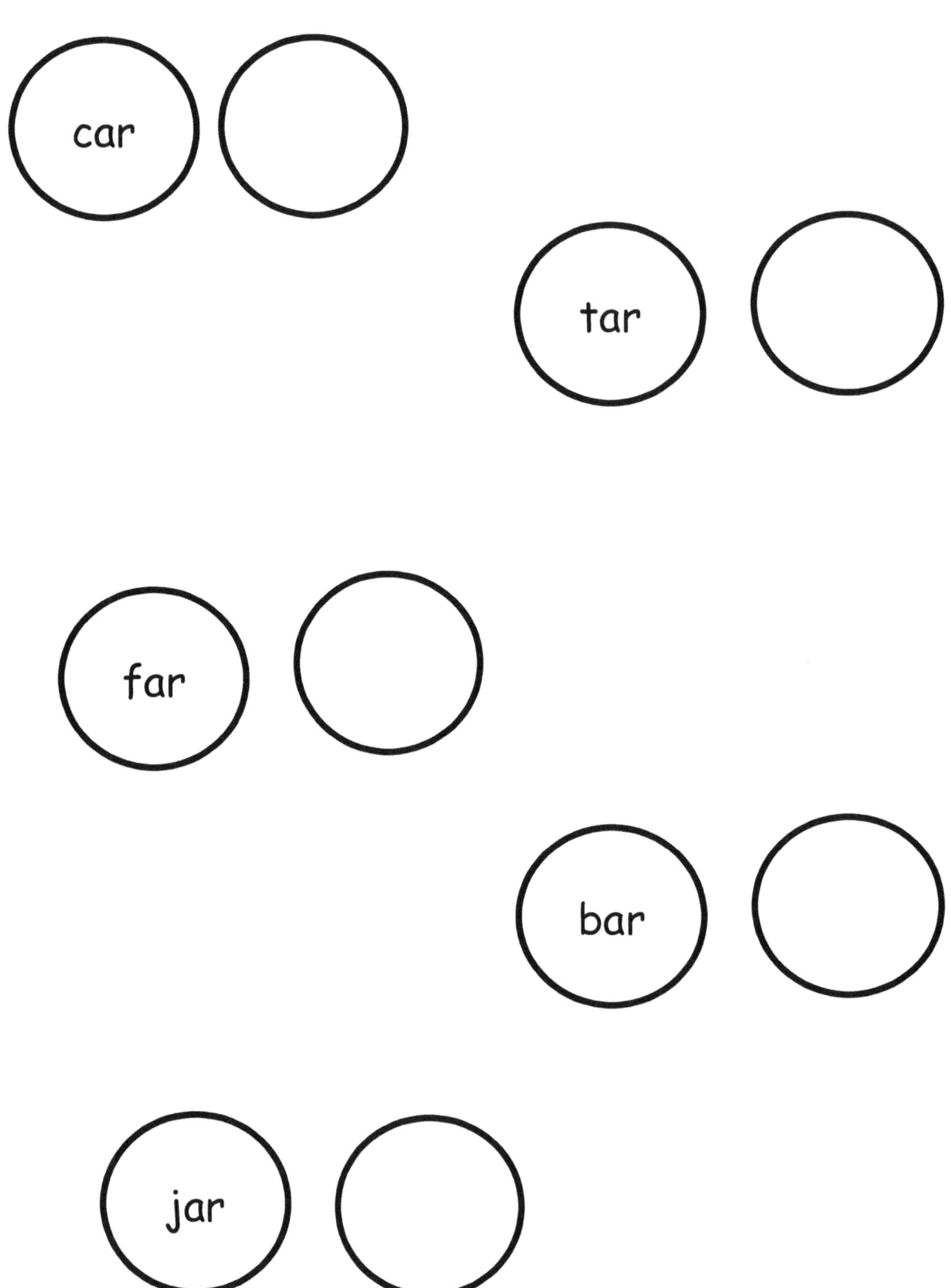

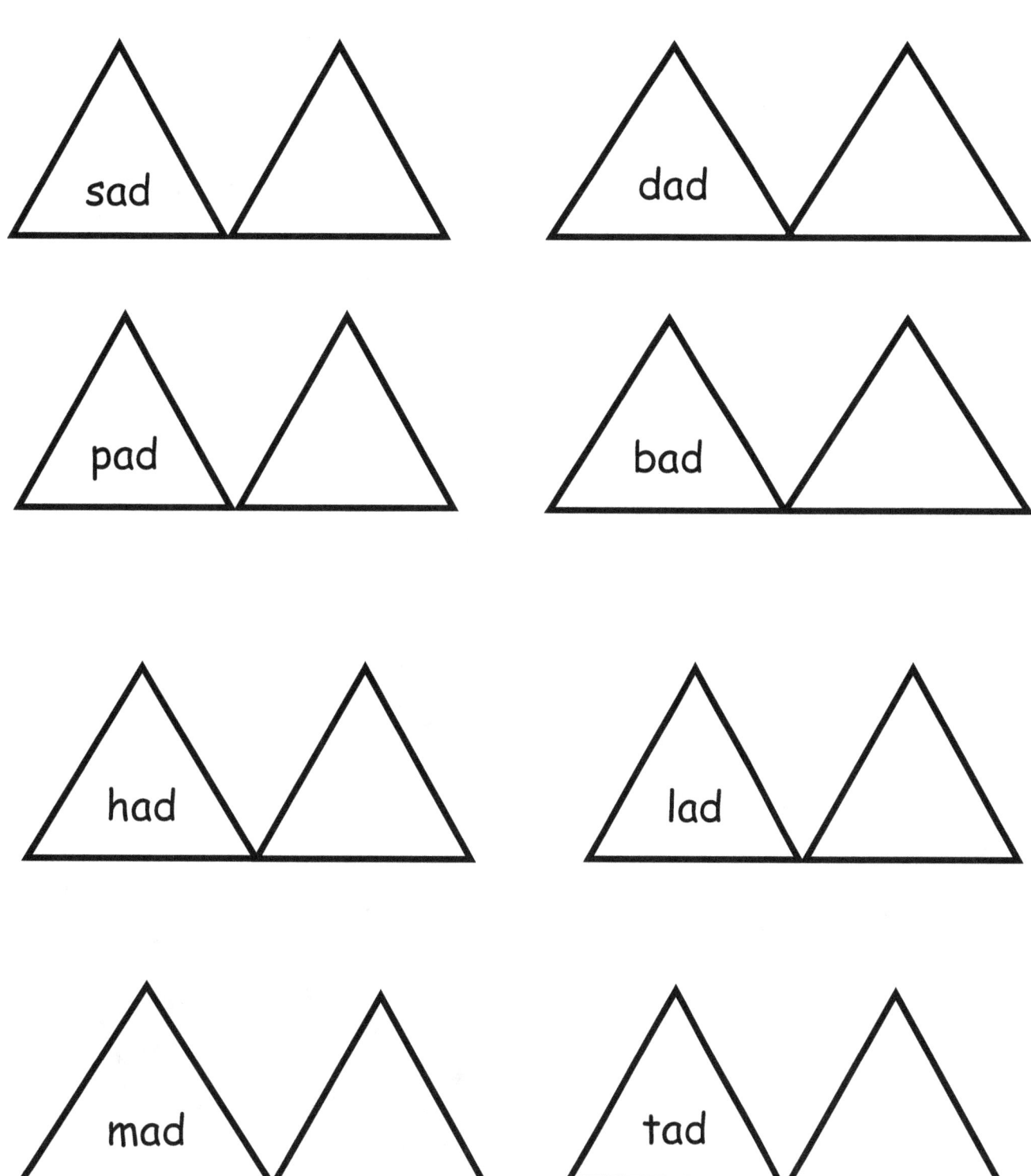

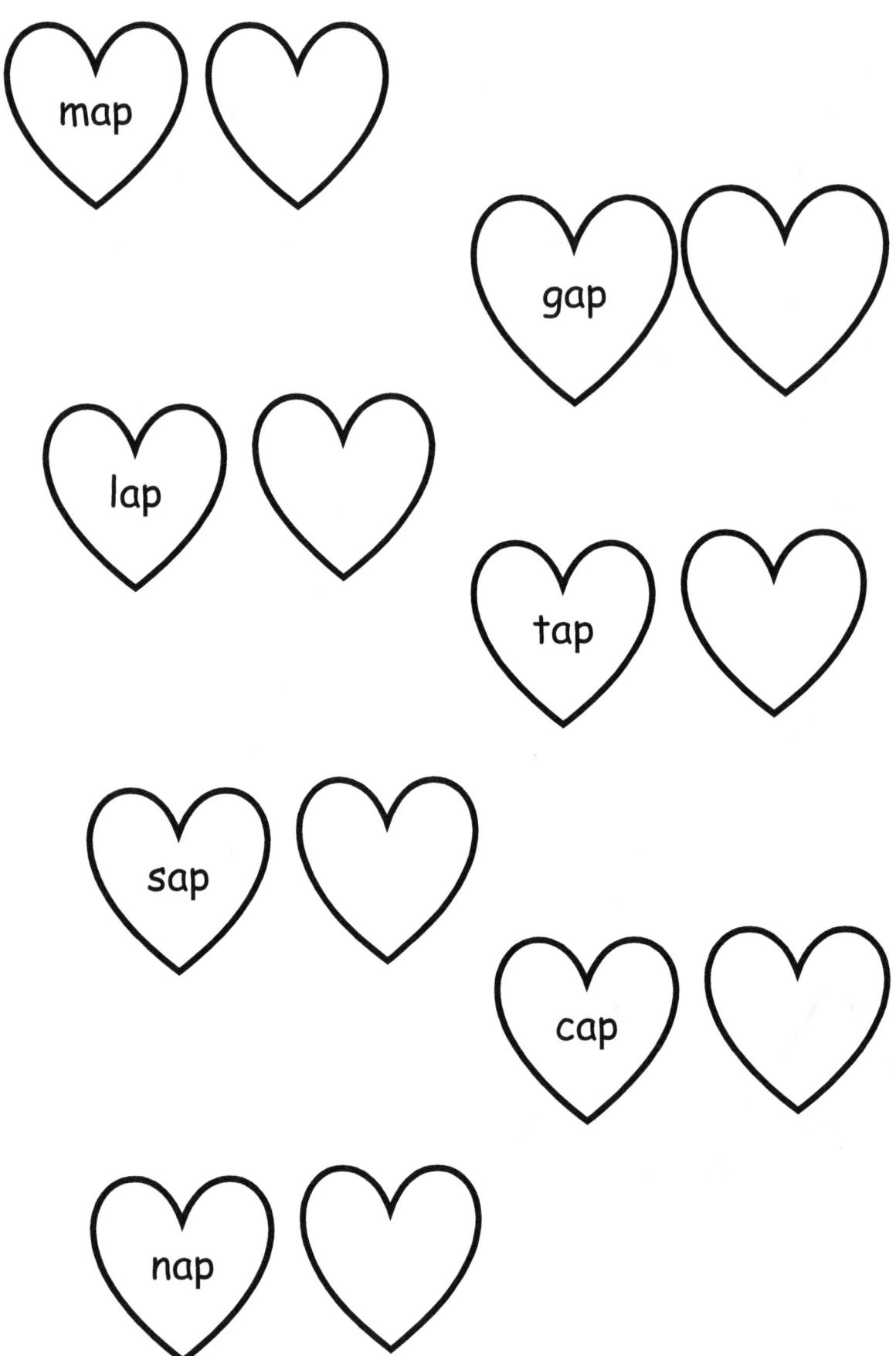

| set | |

| | bet | |

| let | |

| | wet | |

| jet | |

| | met | |

| net | |

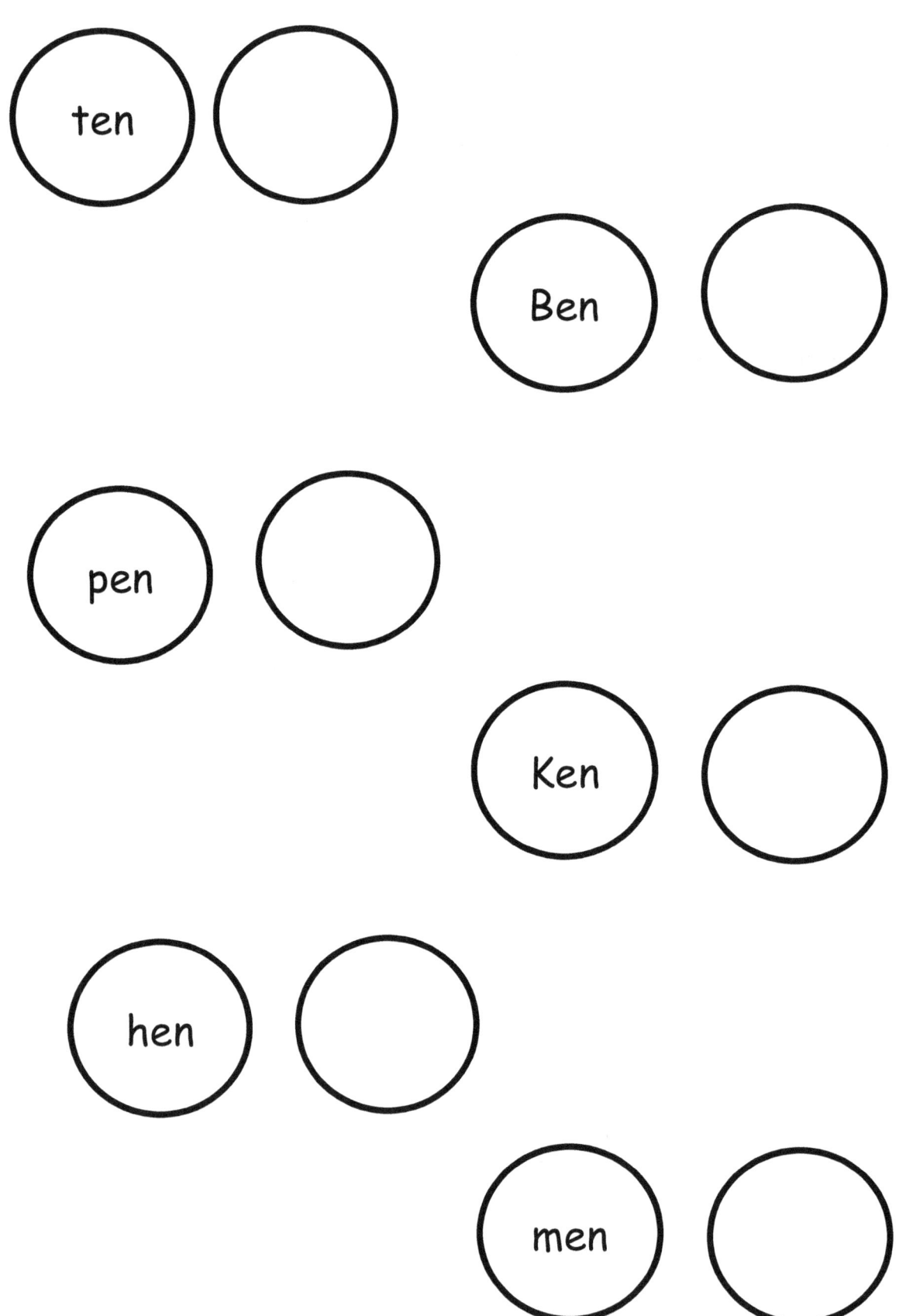

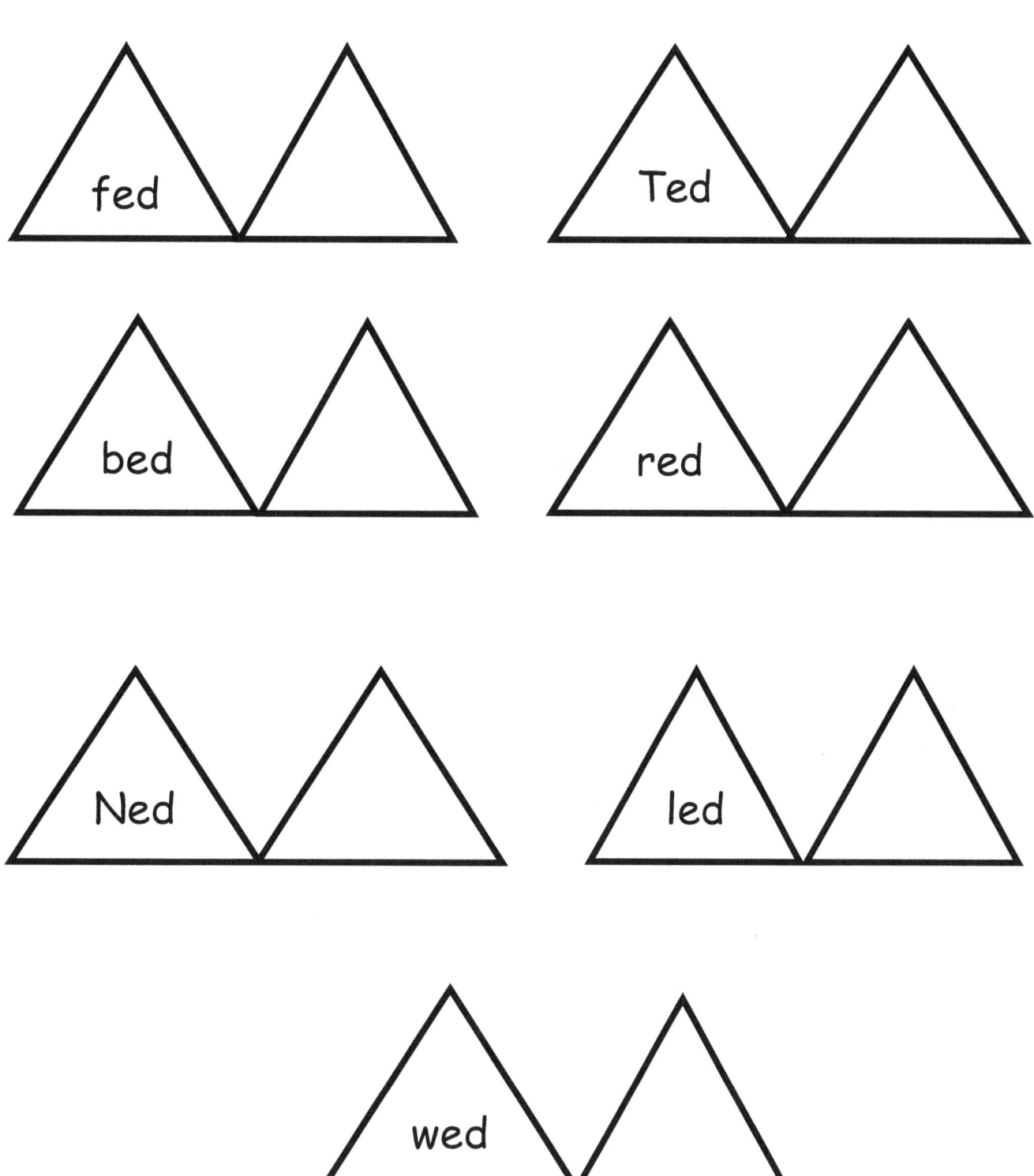

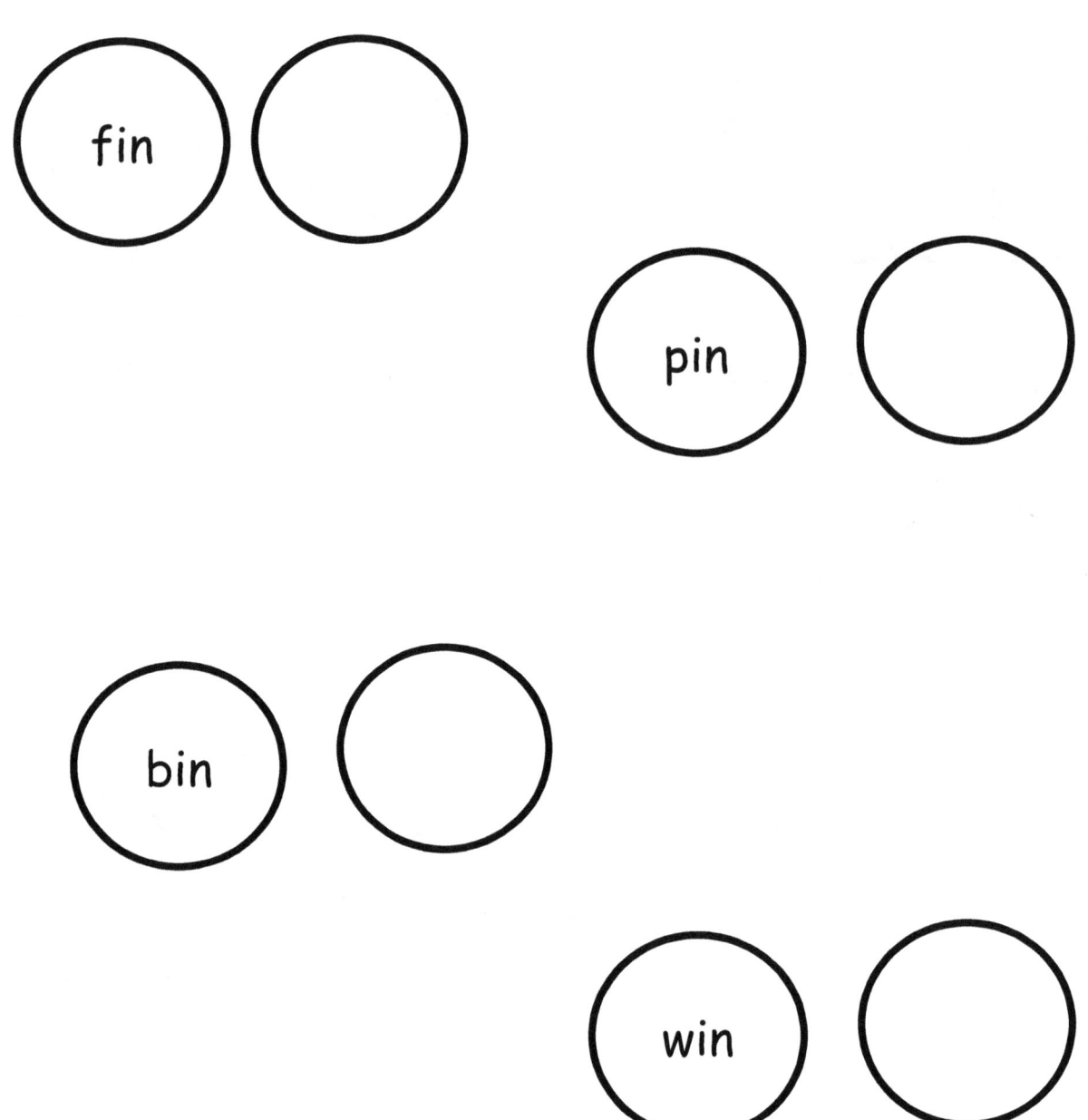

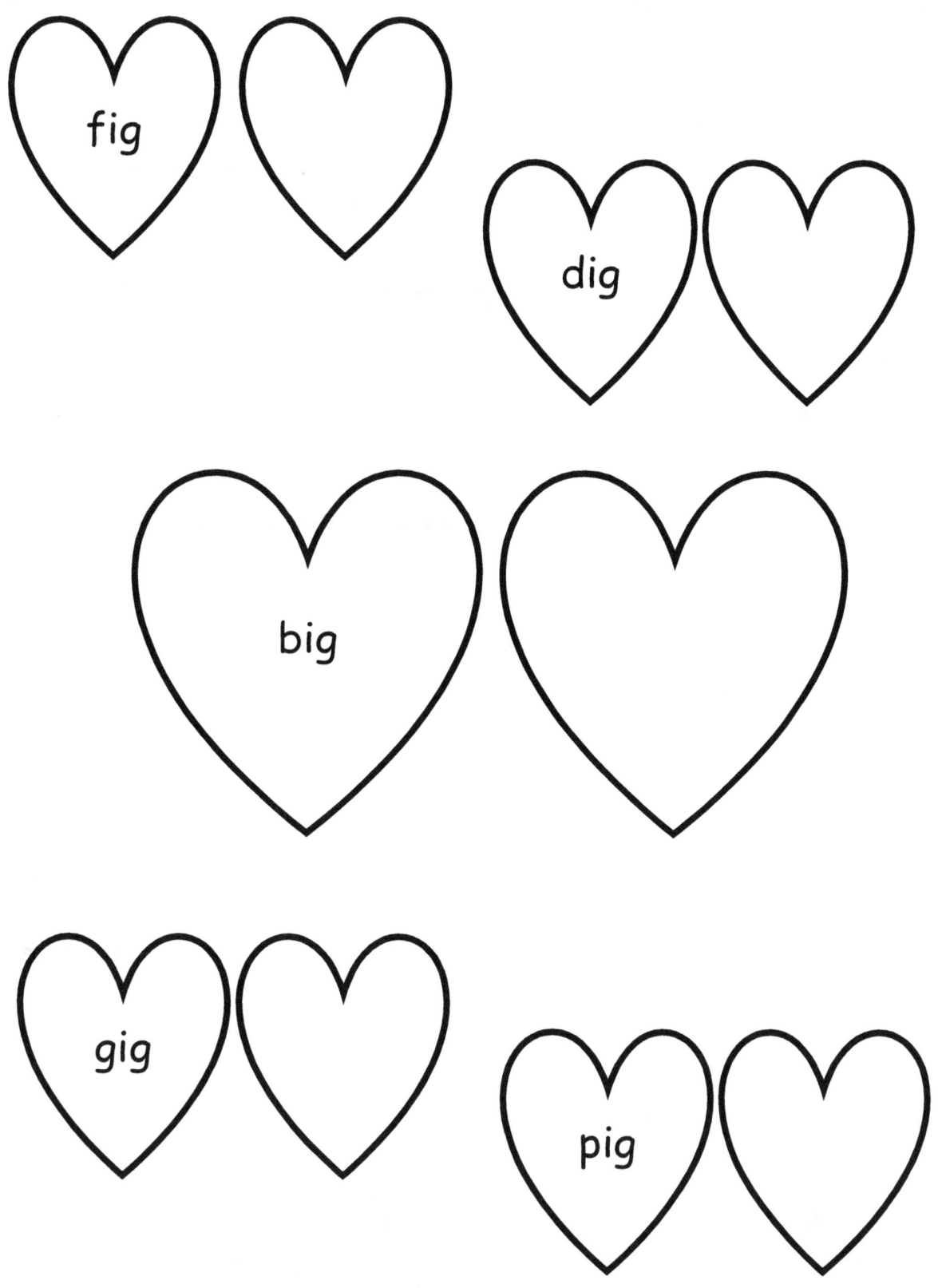

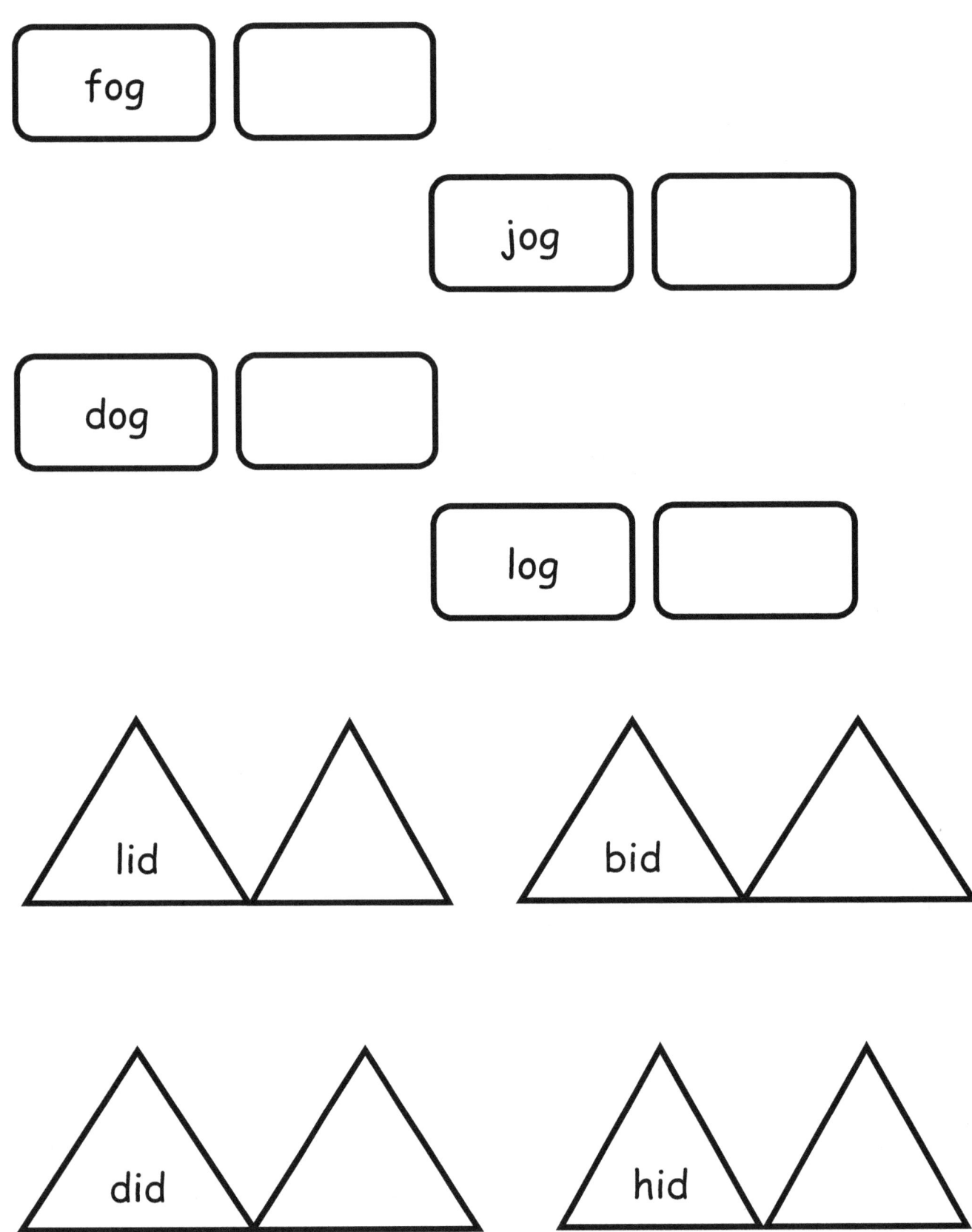

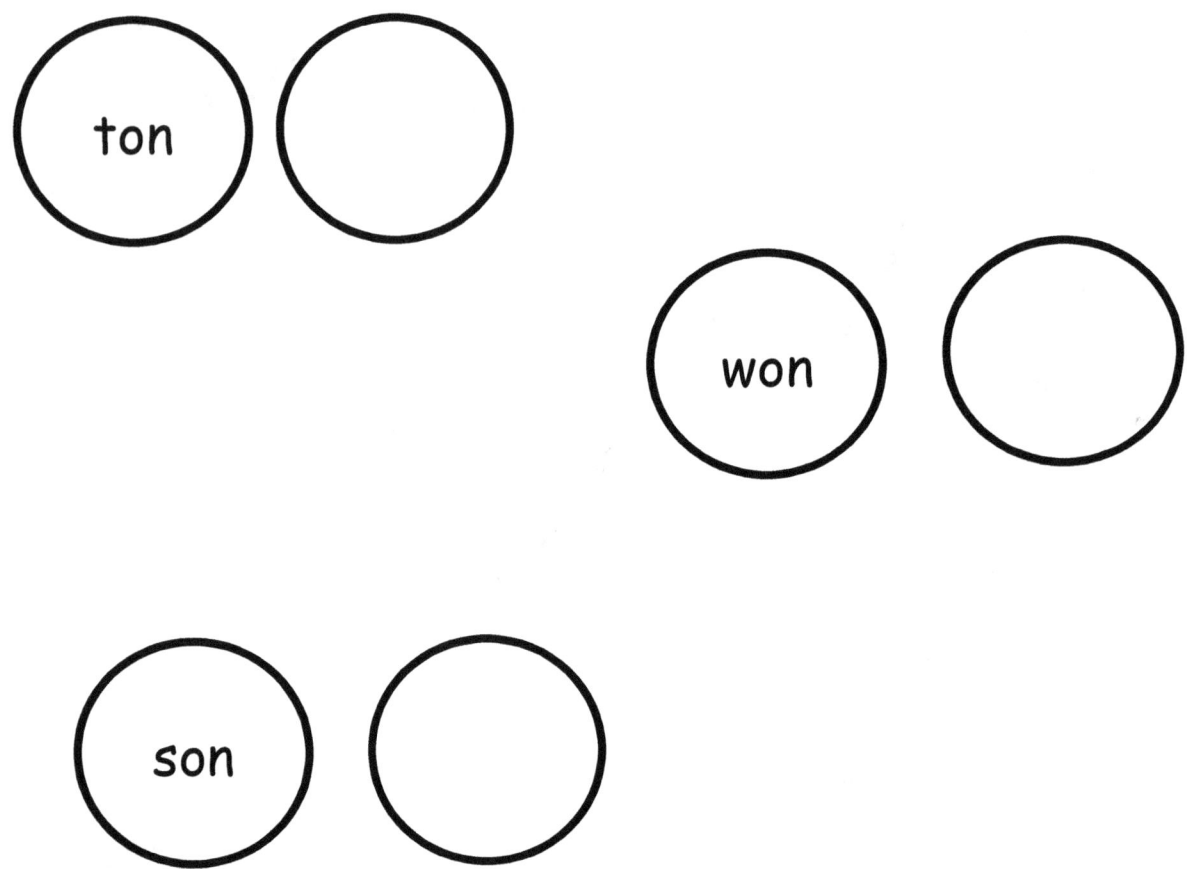

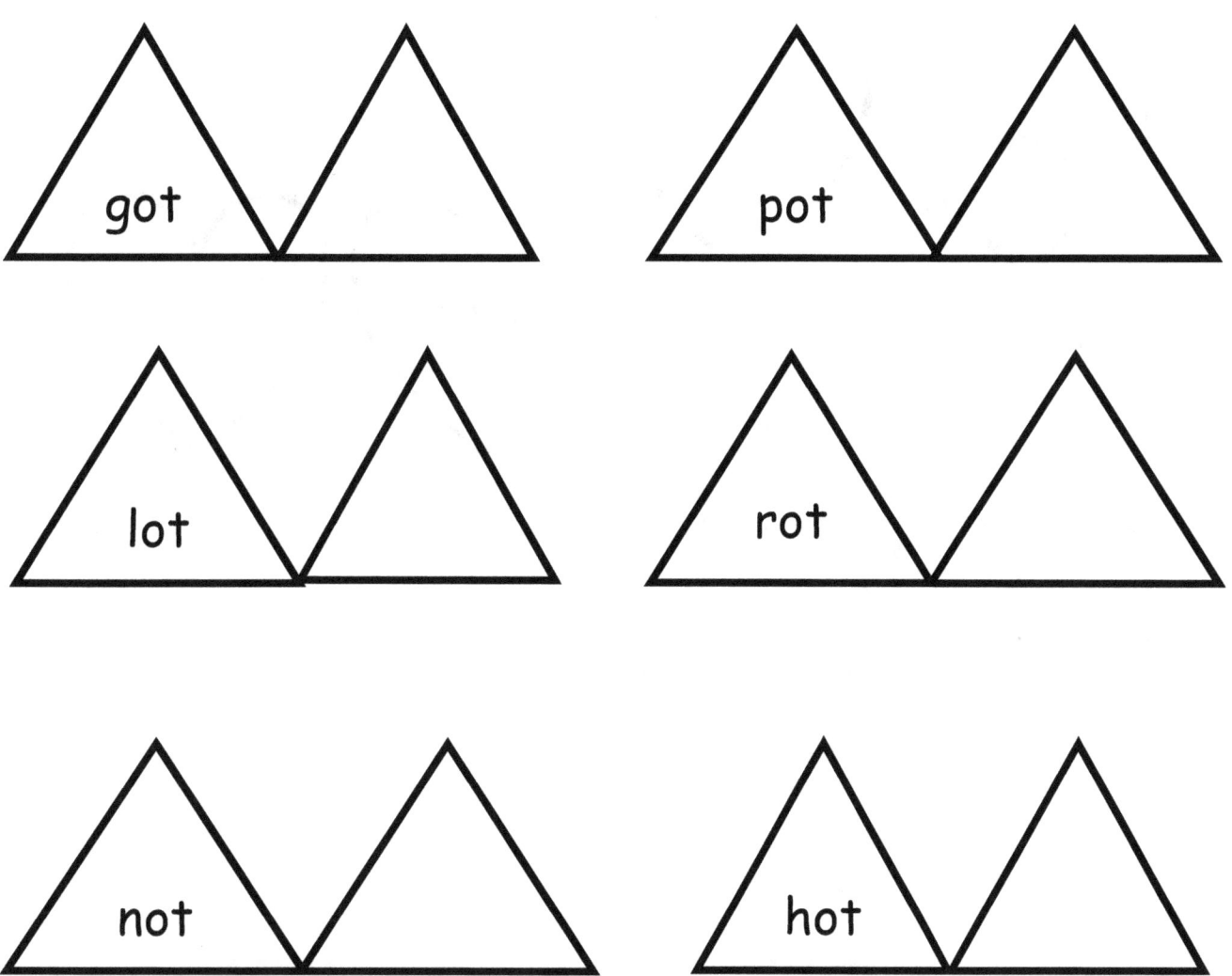

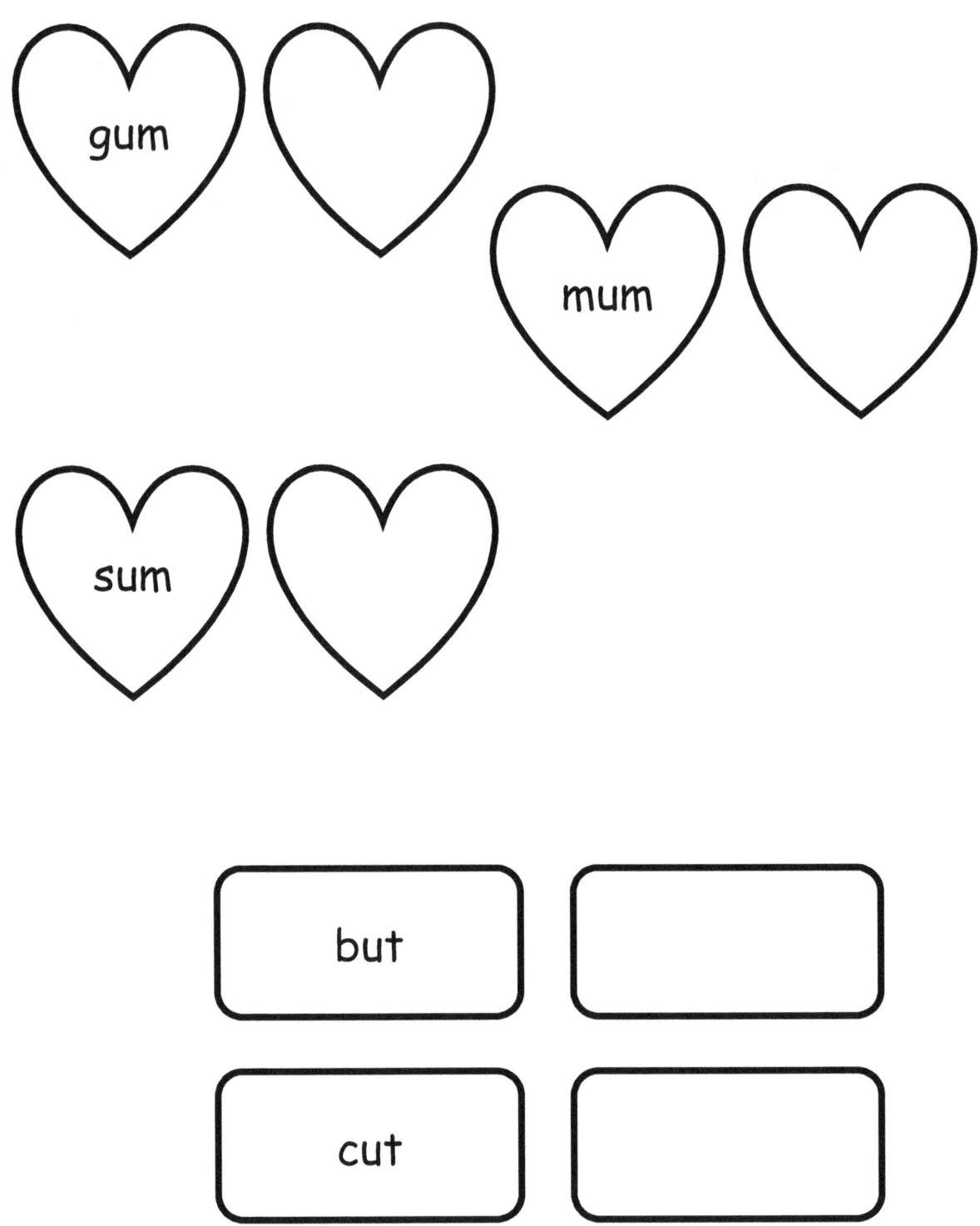

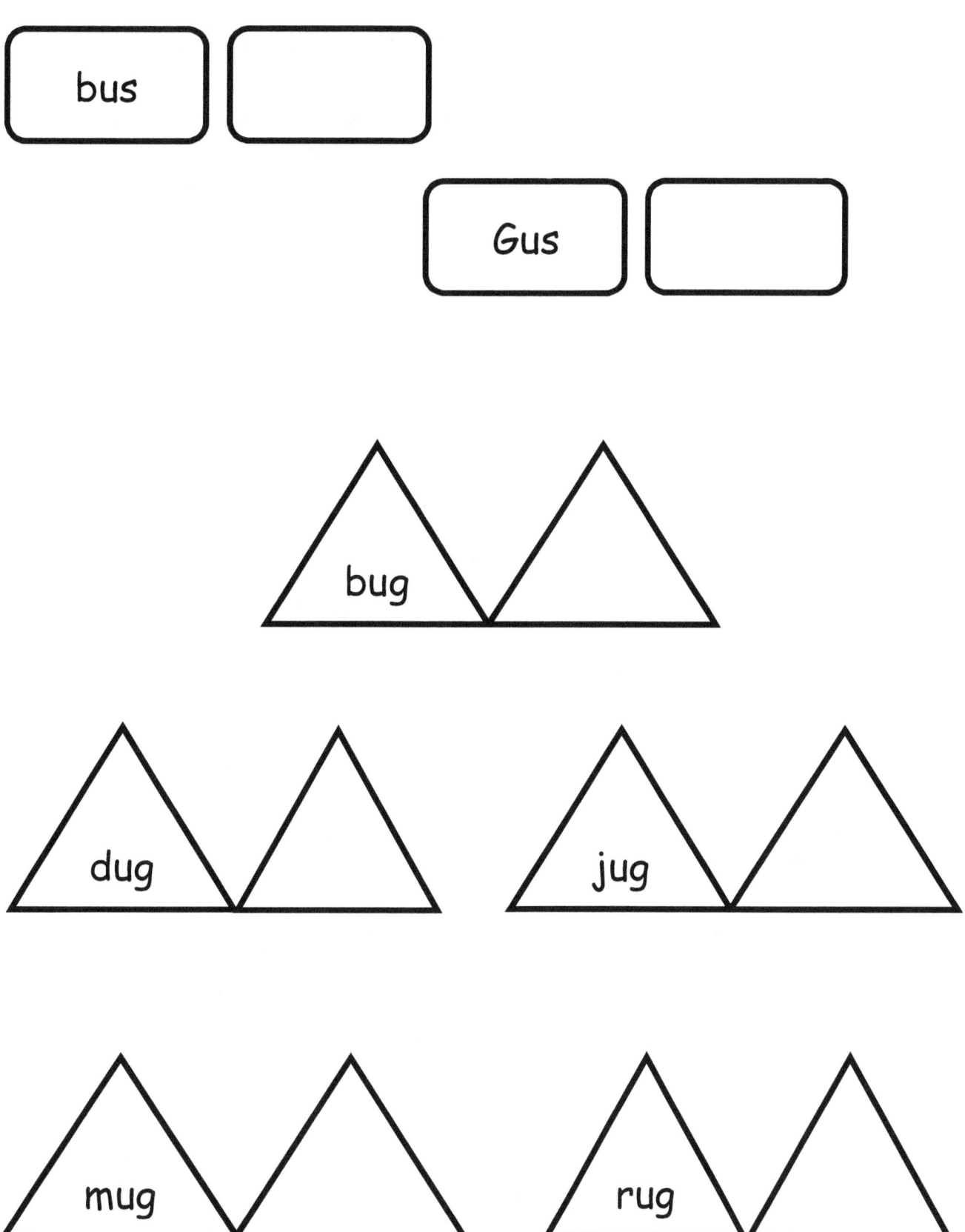

six

see

bee

mom

Tom

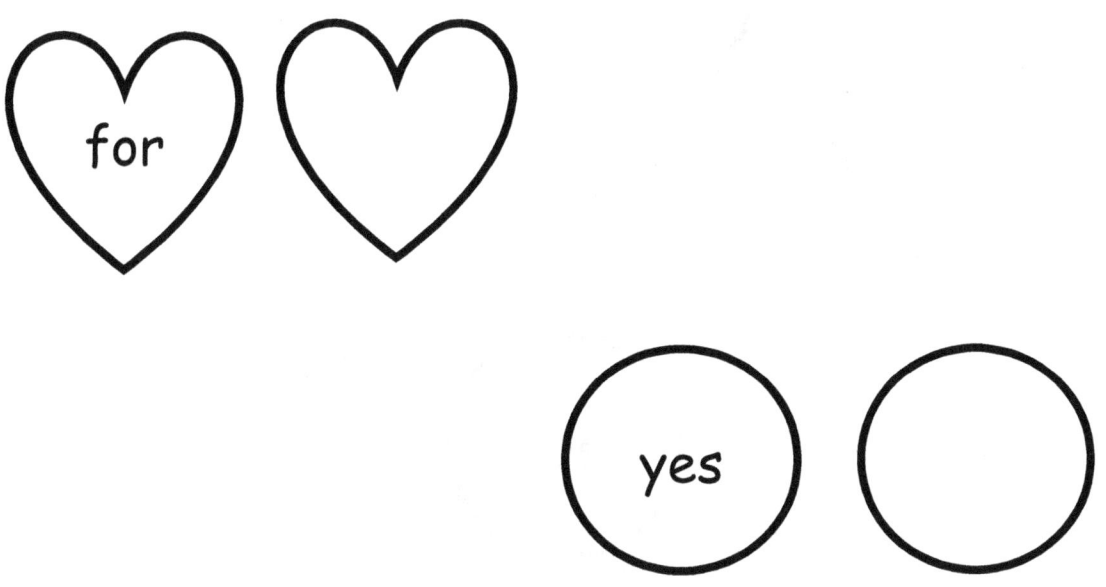

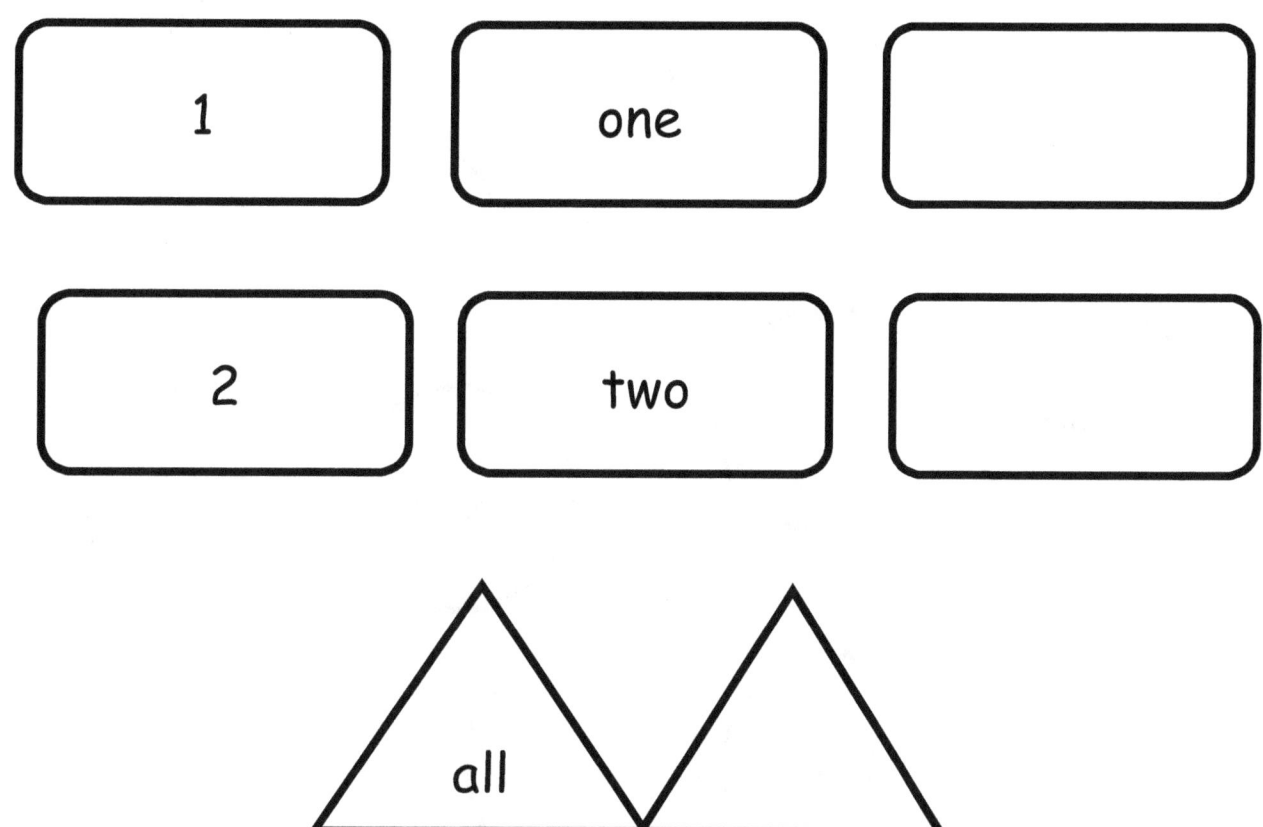

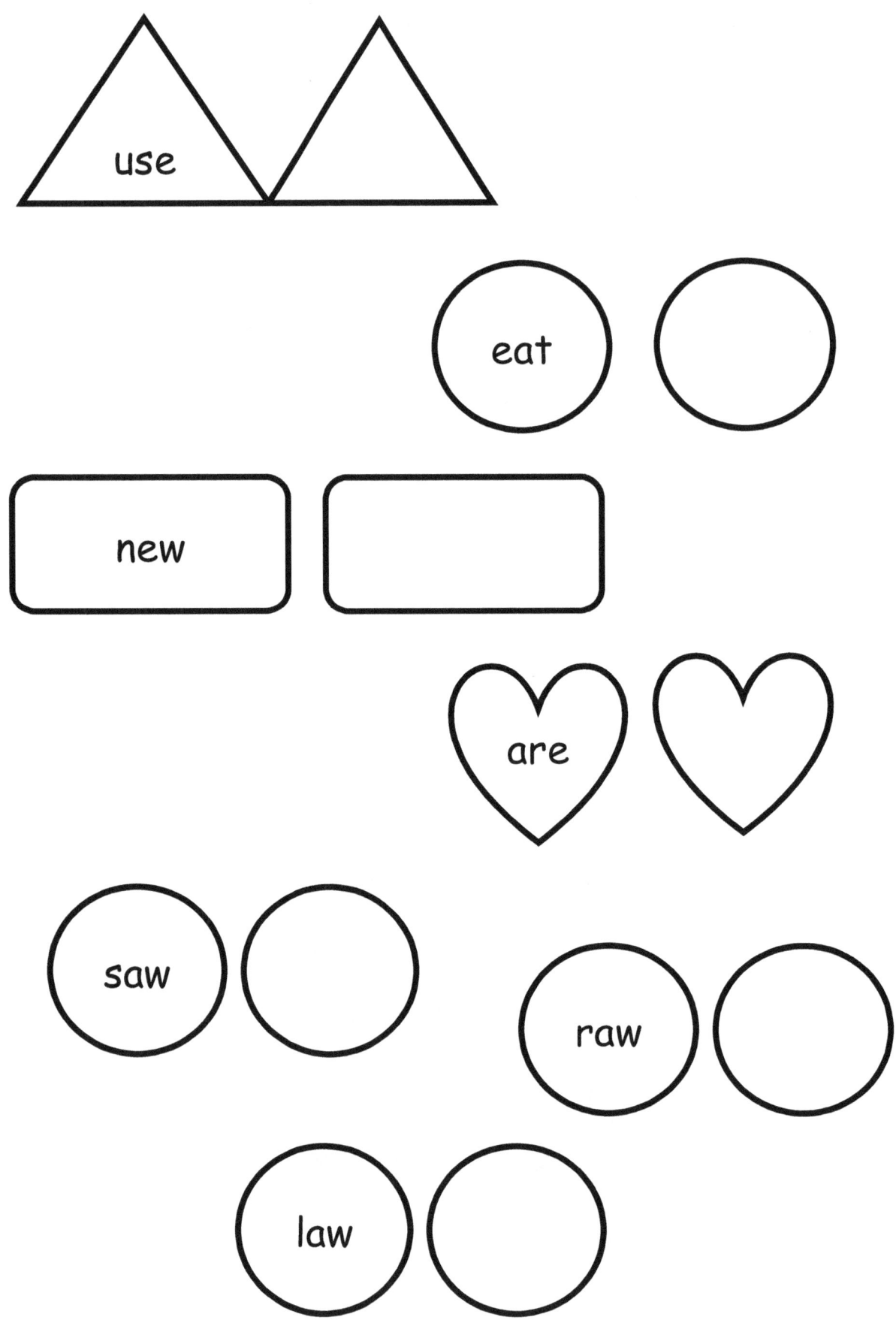

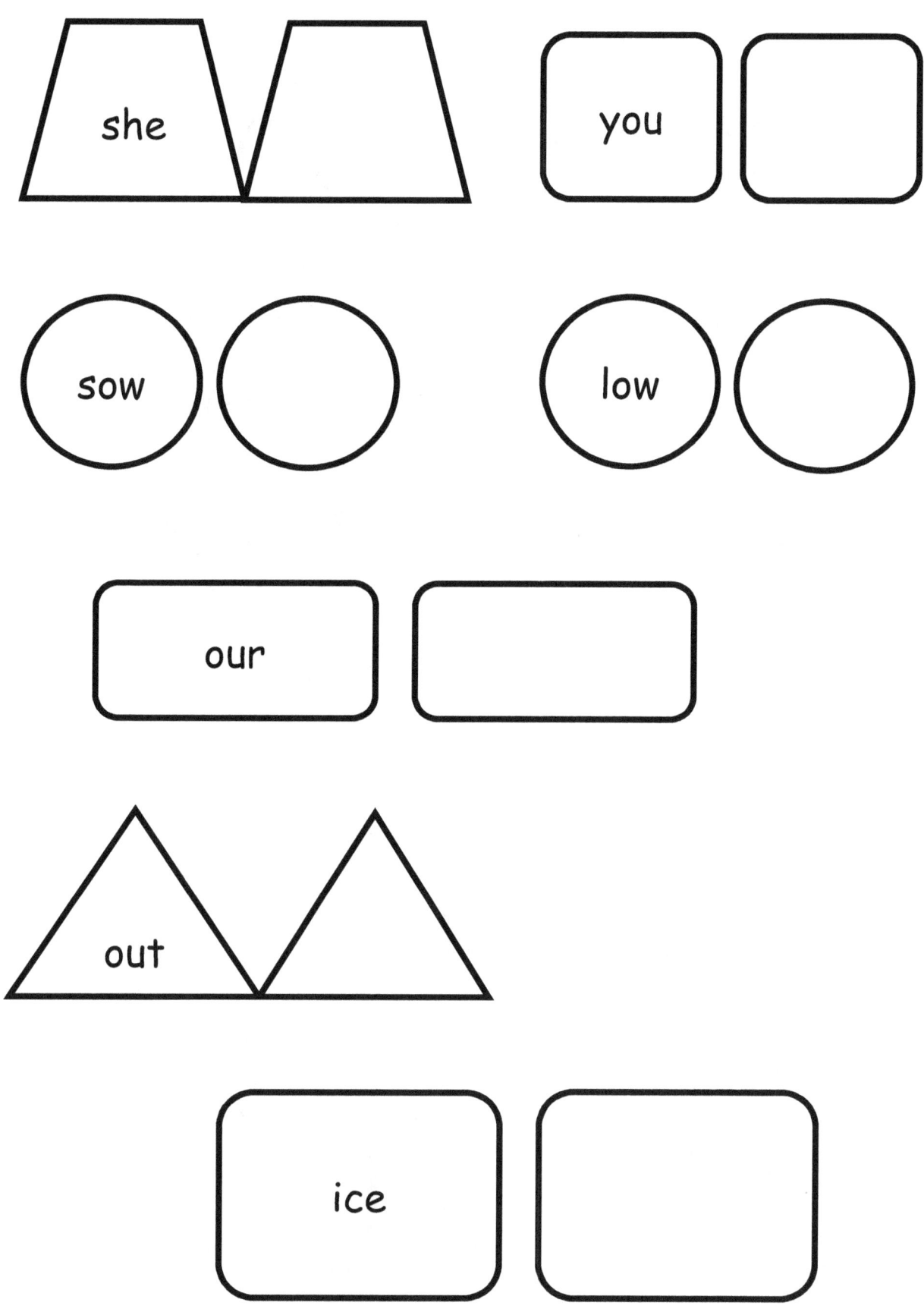

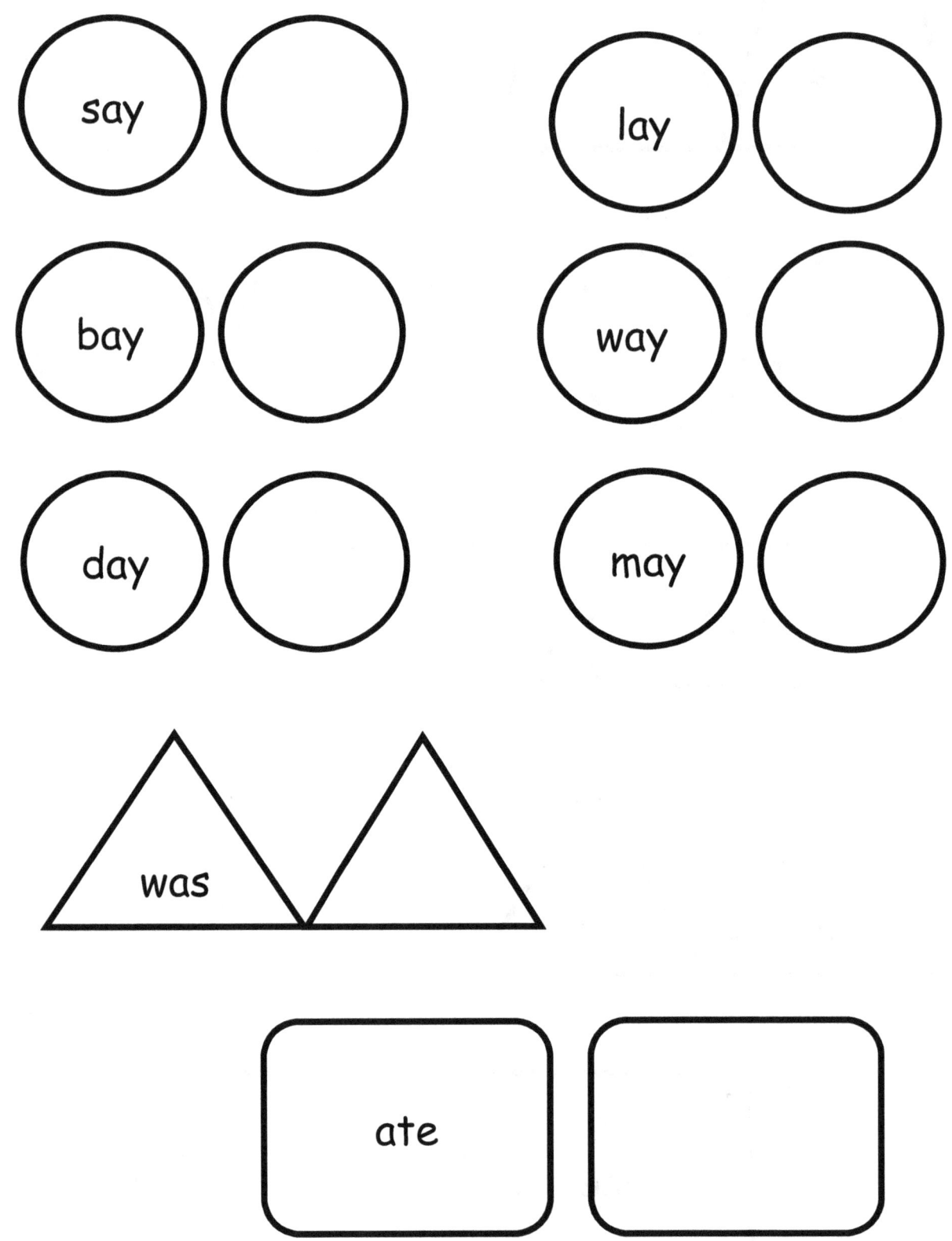

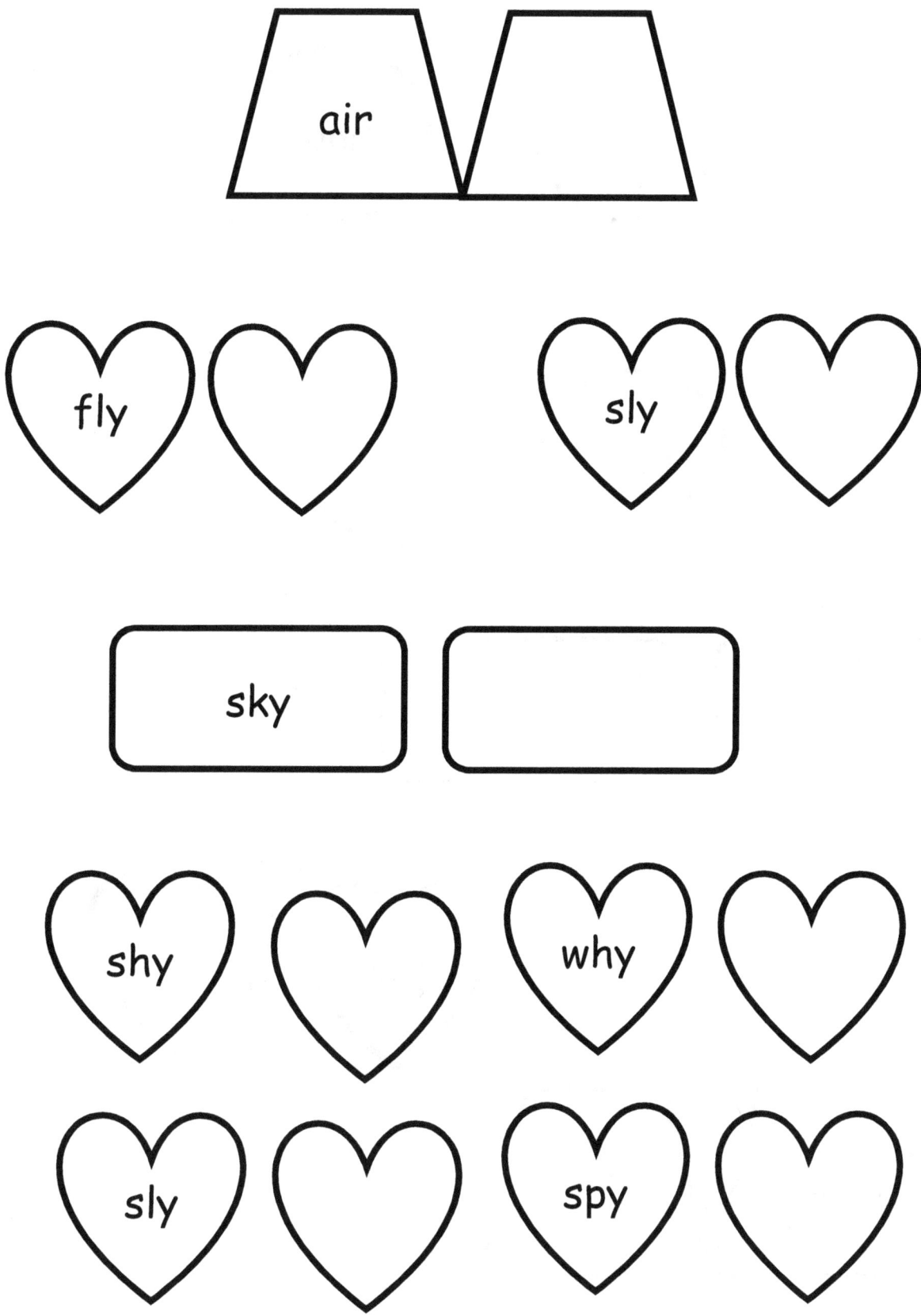

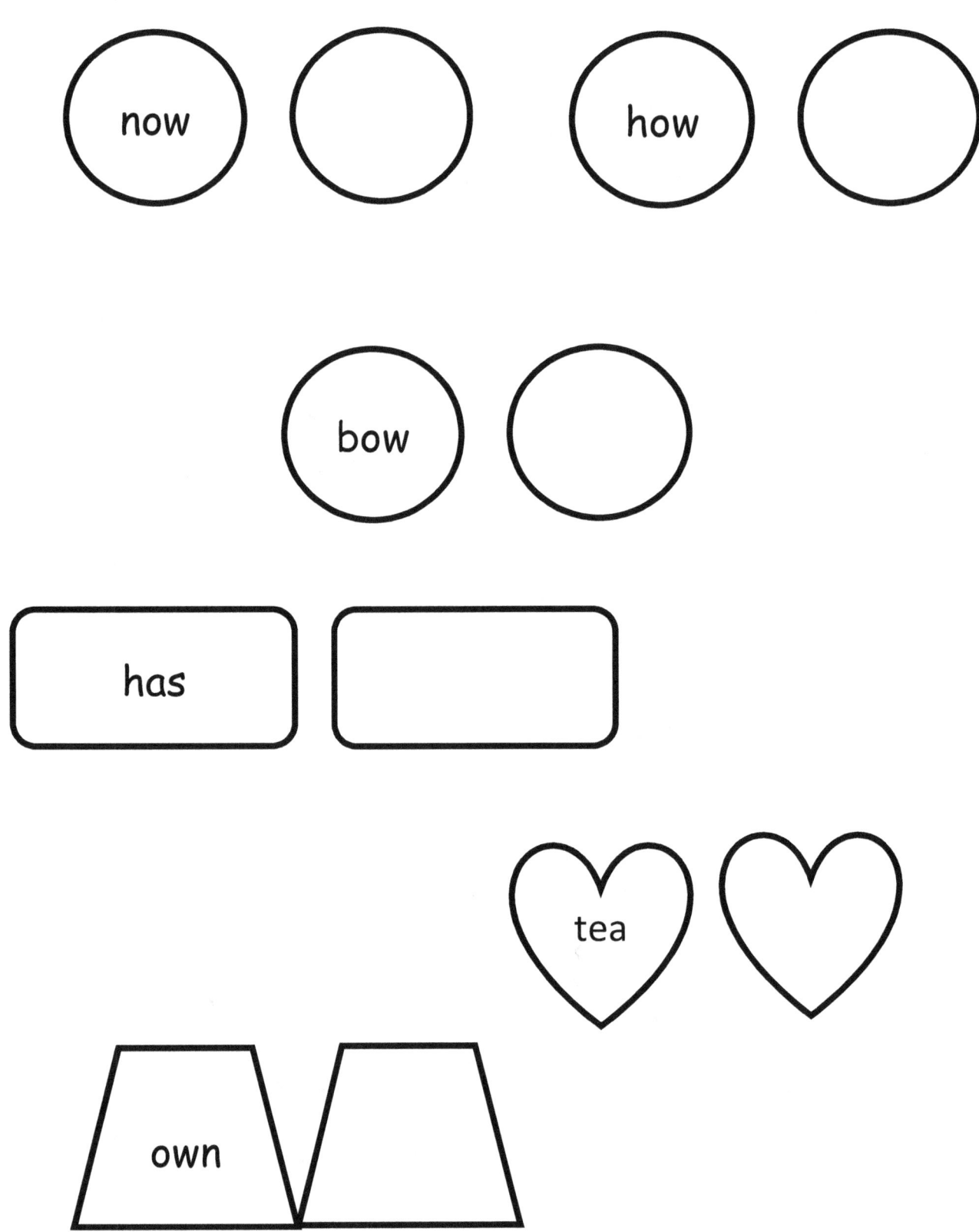

Let us read every day

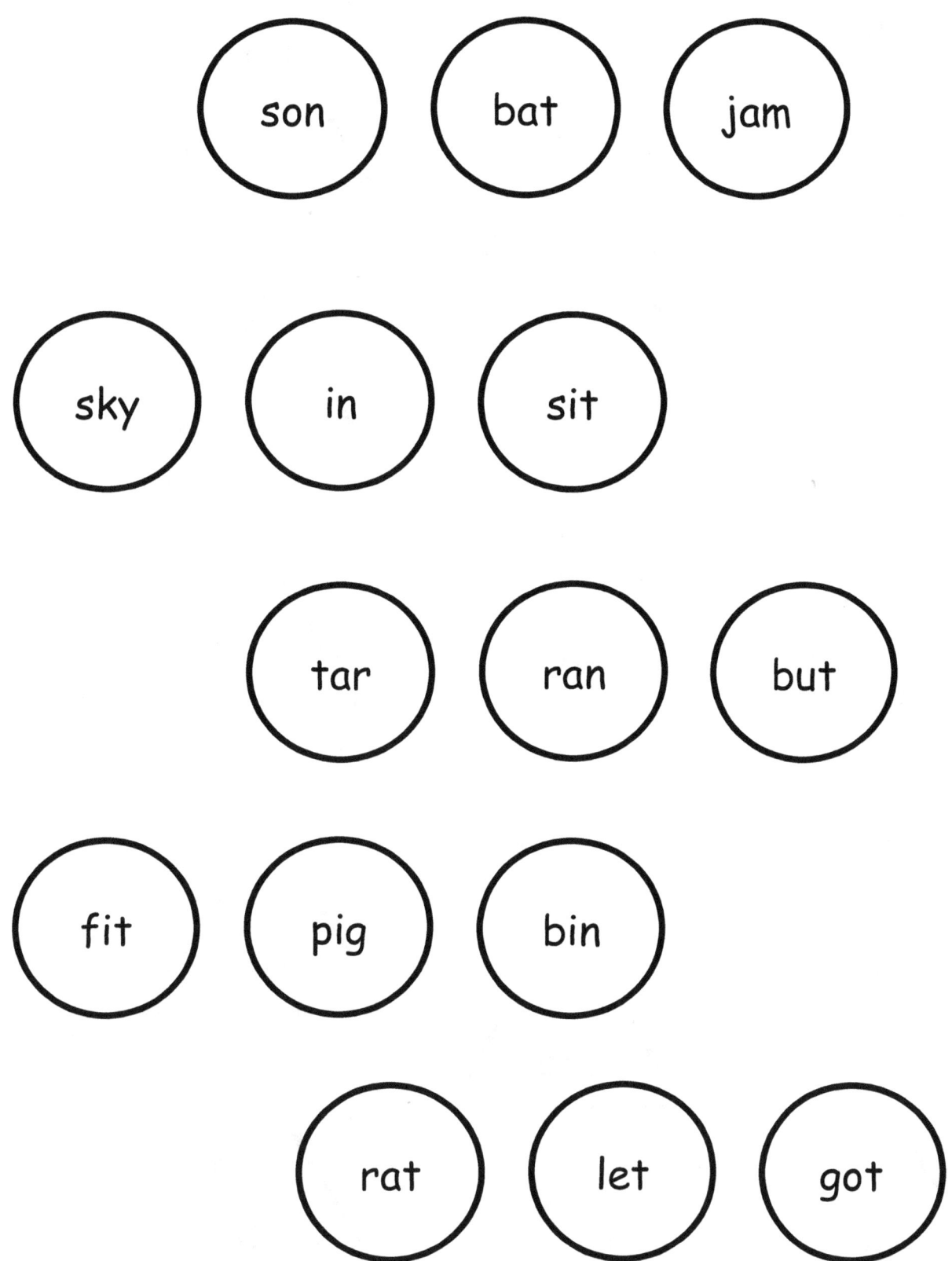

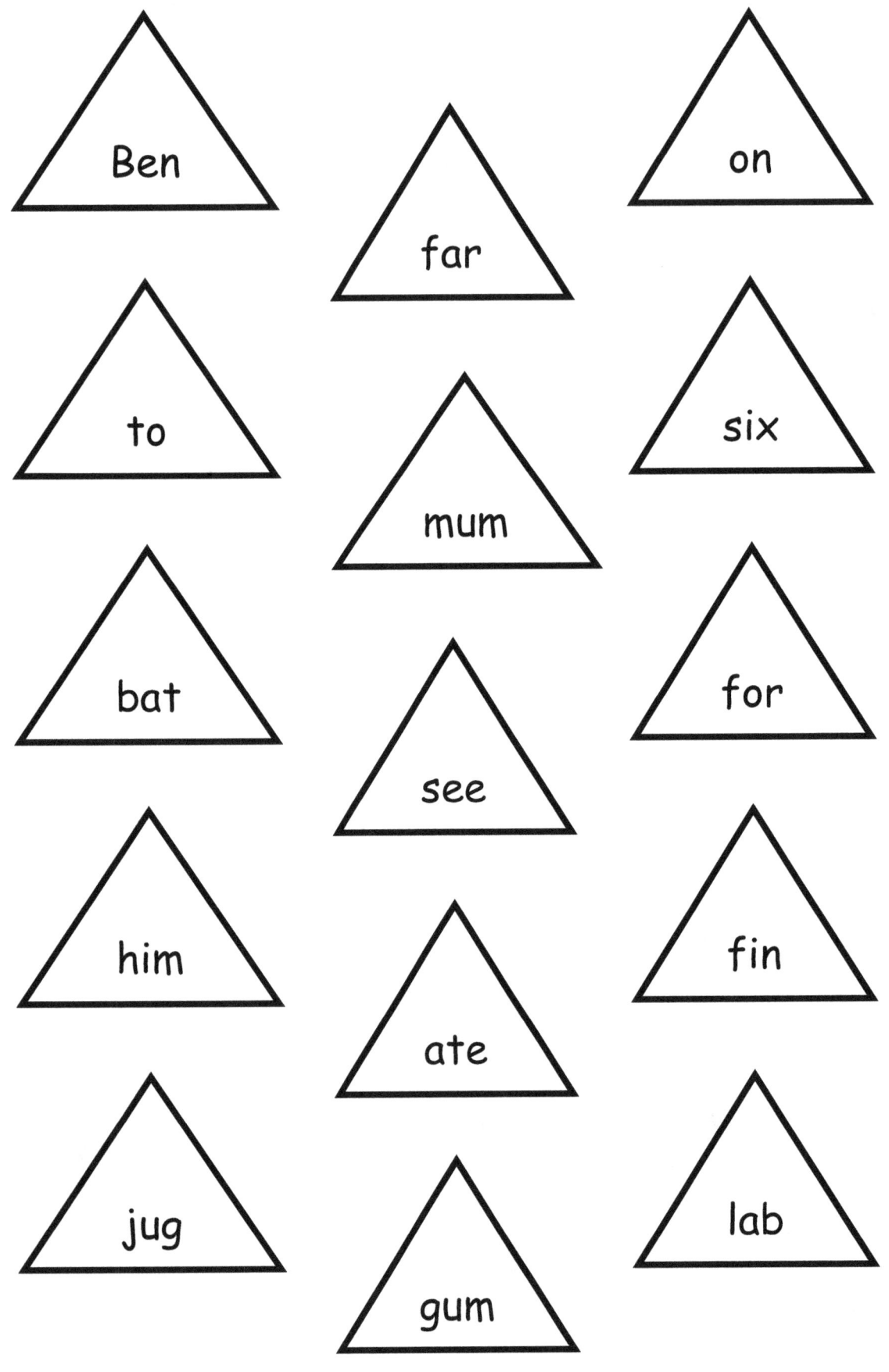

art	fat	Pam
sip	no	peg
gum	are	but
fit	fig	fin
ant	leg	get

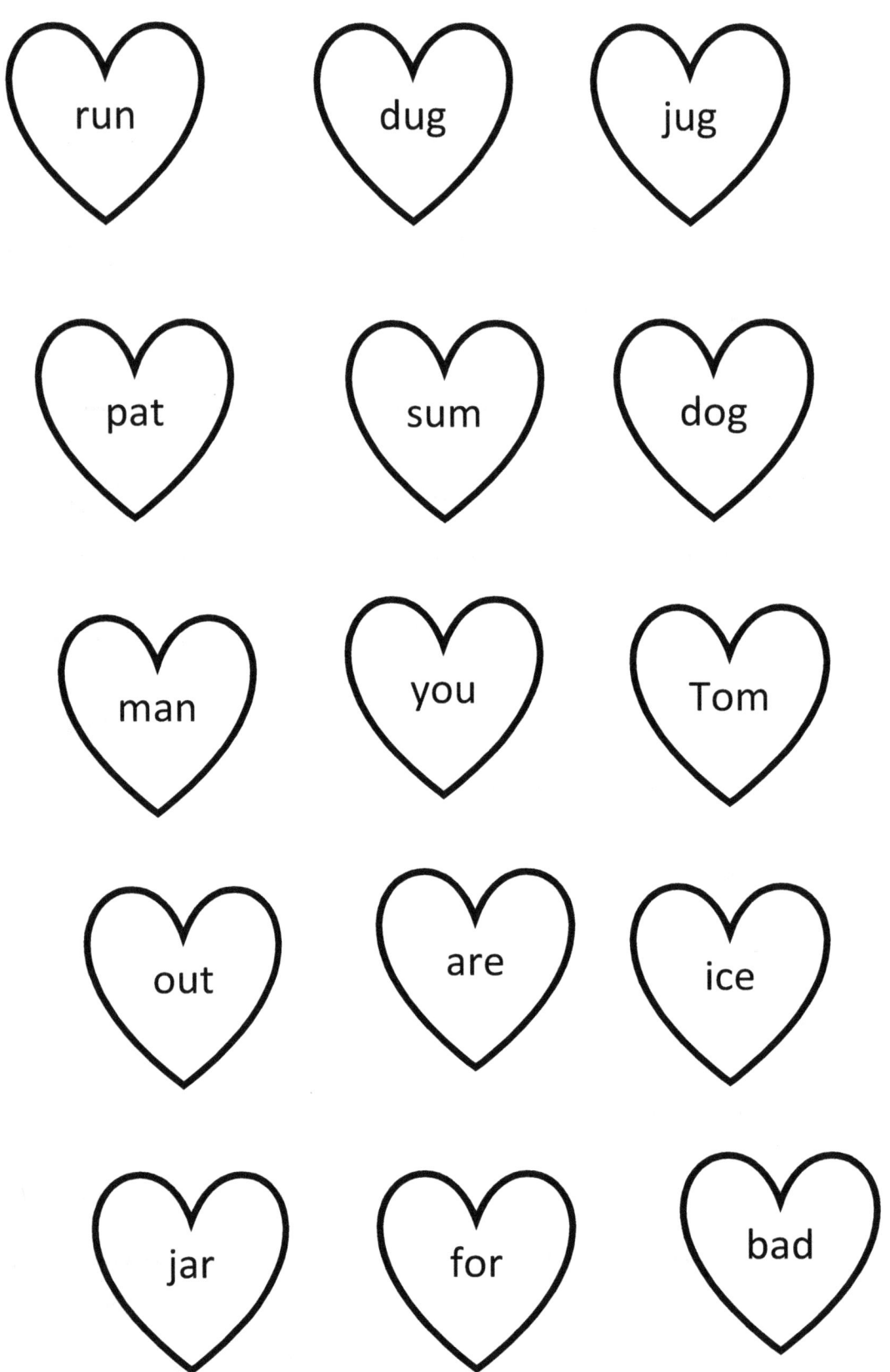

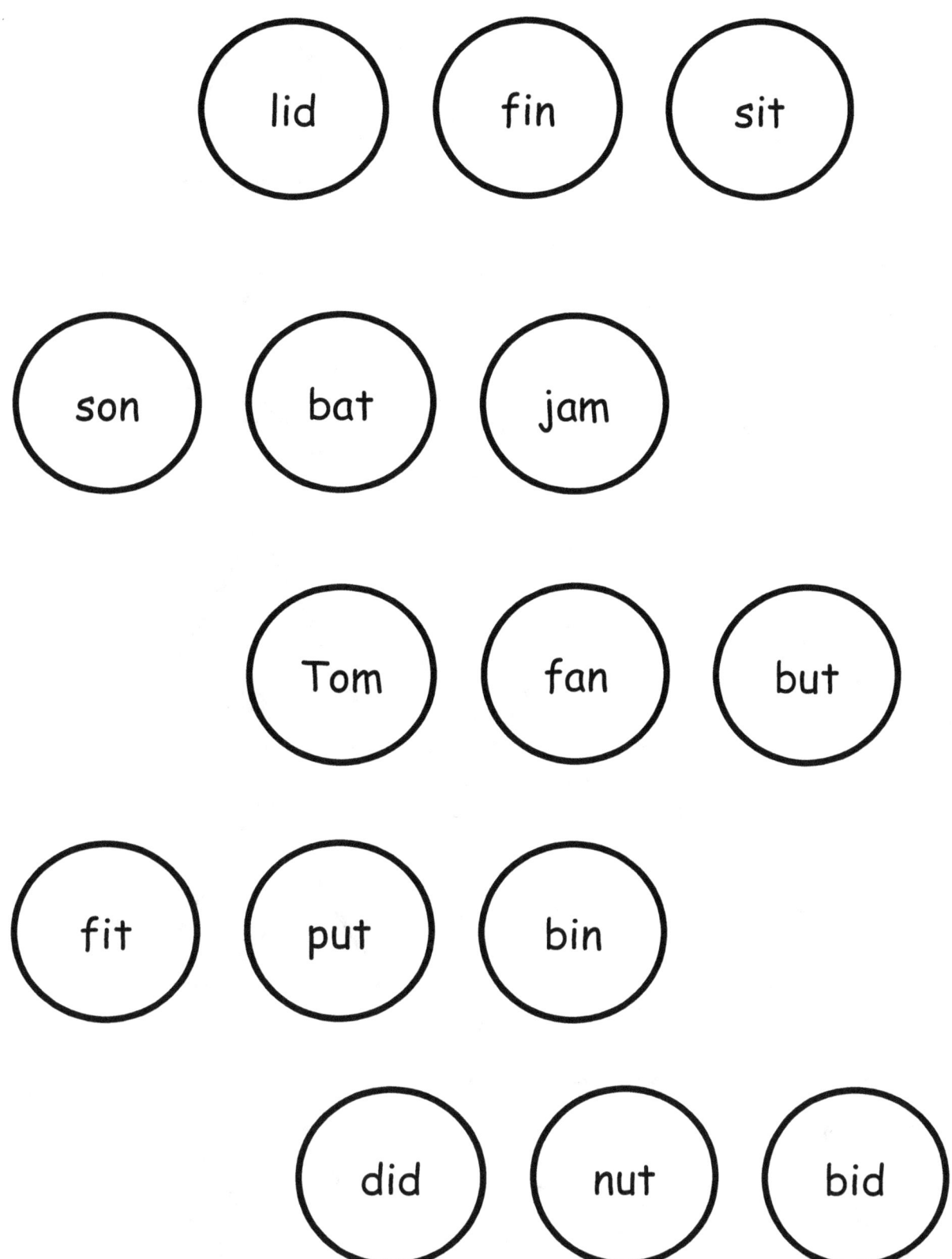

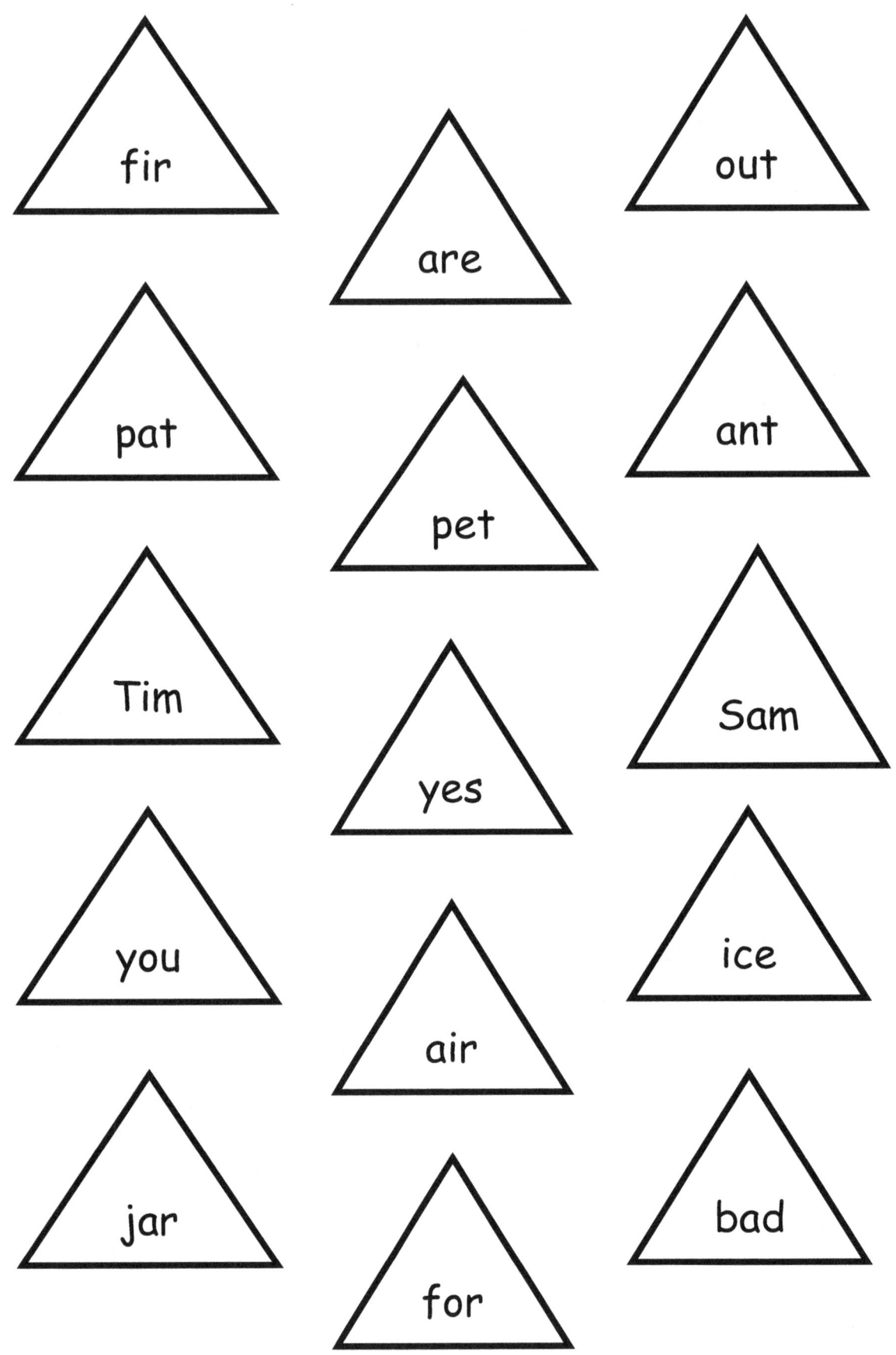

on	ham	did
yet	hit	wit
yet	hit	wit
it	two	bit
Sid	sad	had

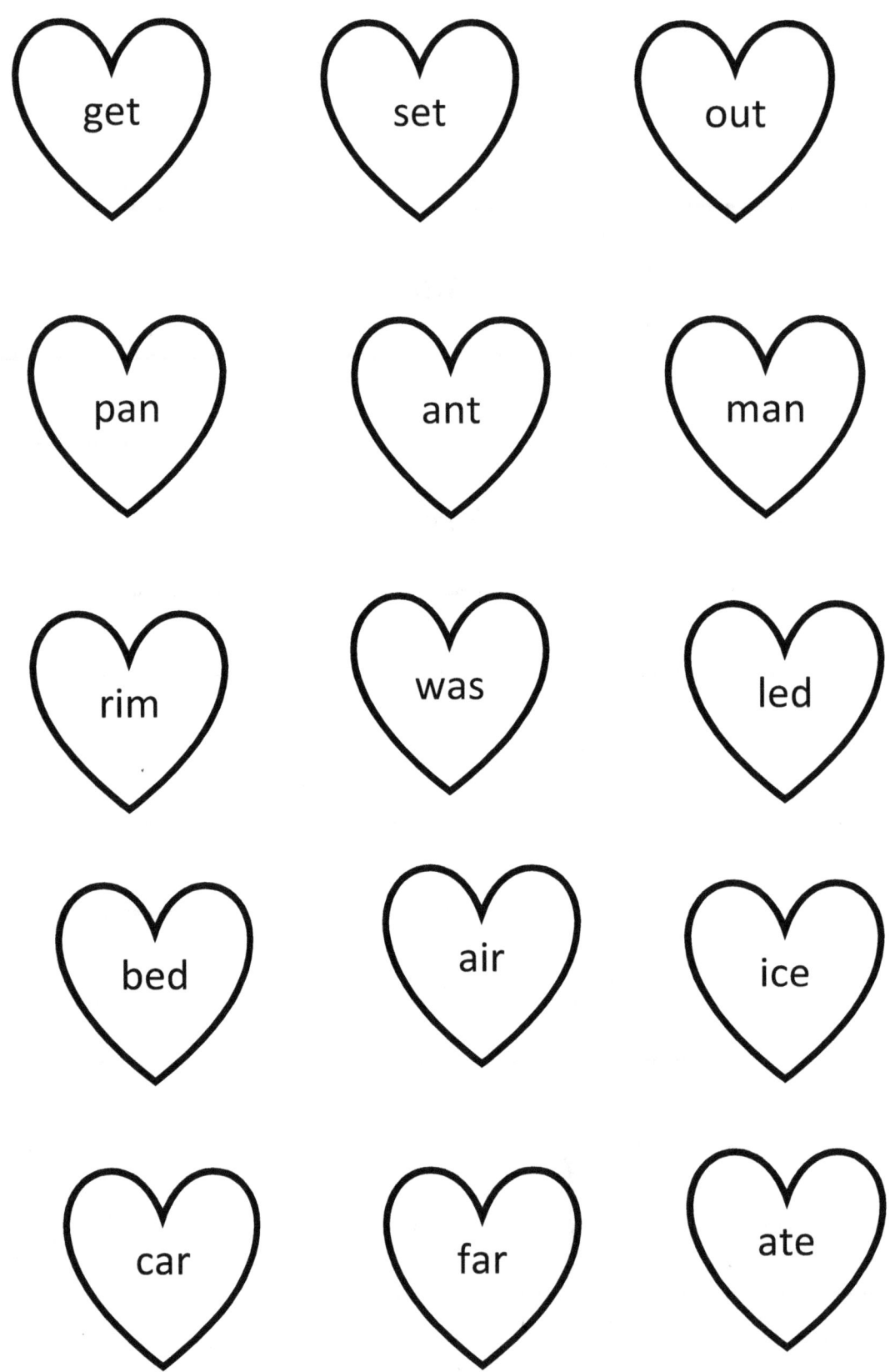

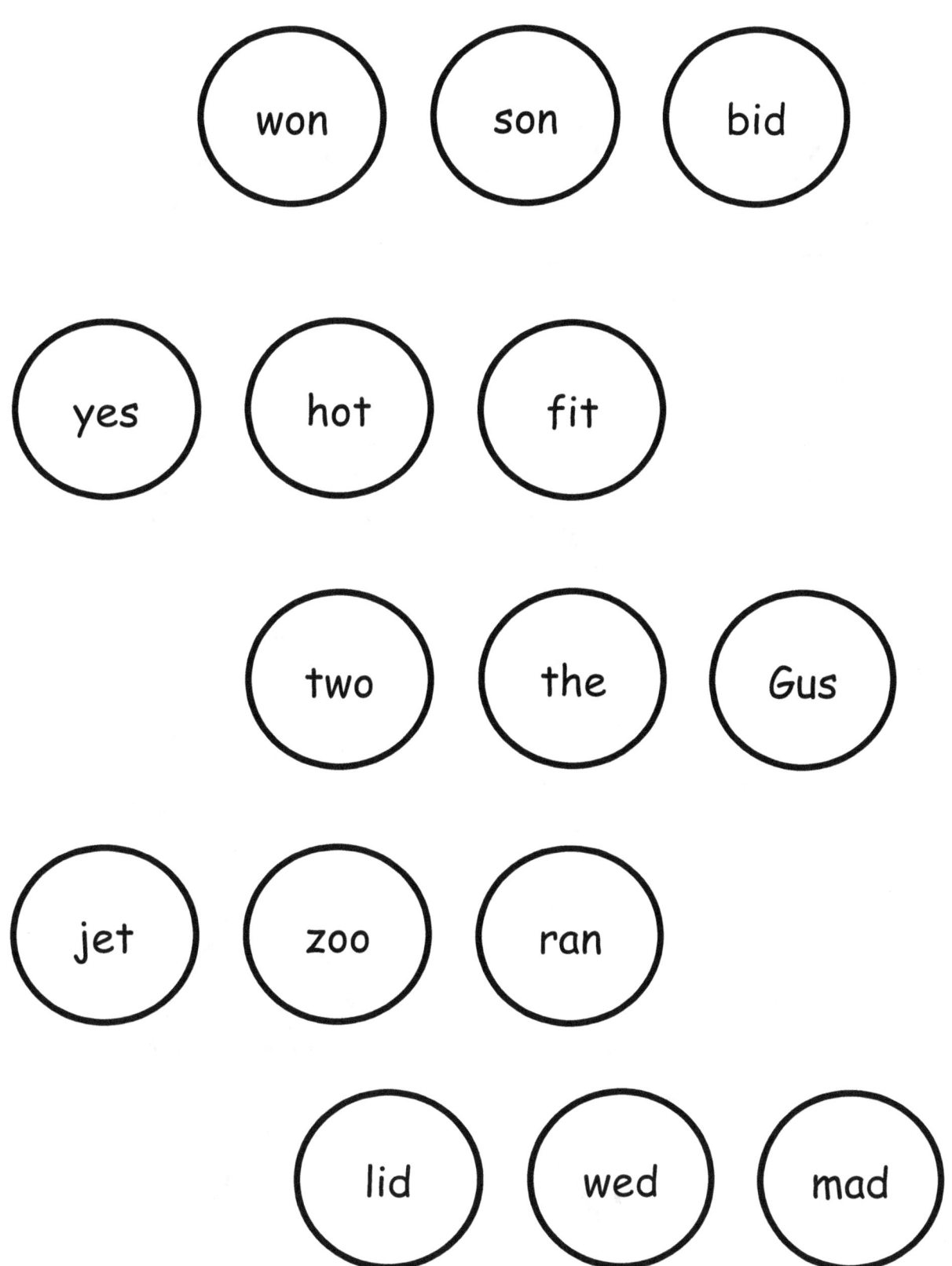

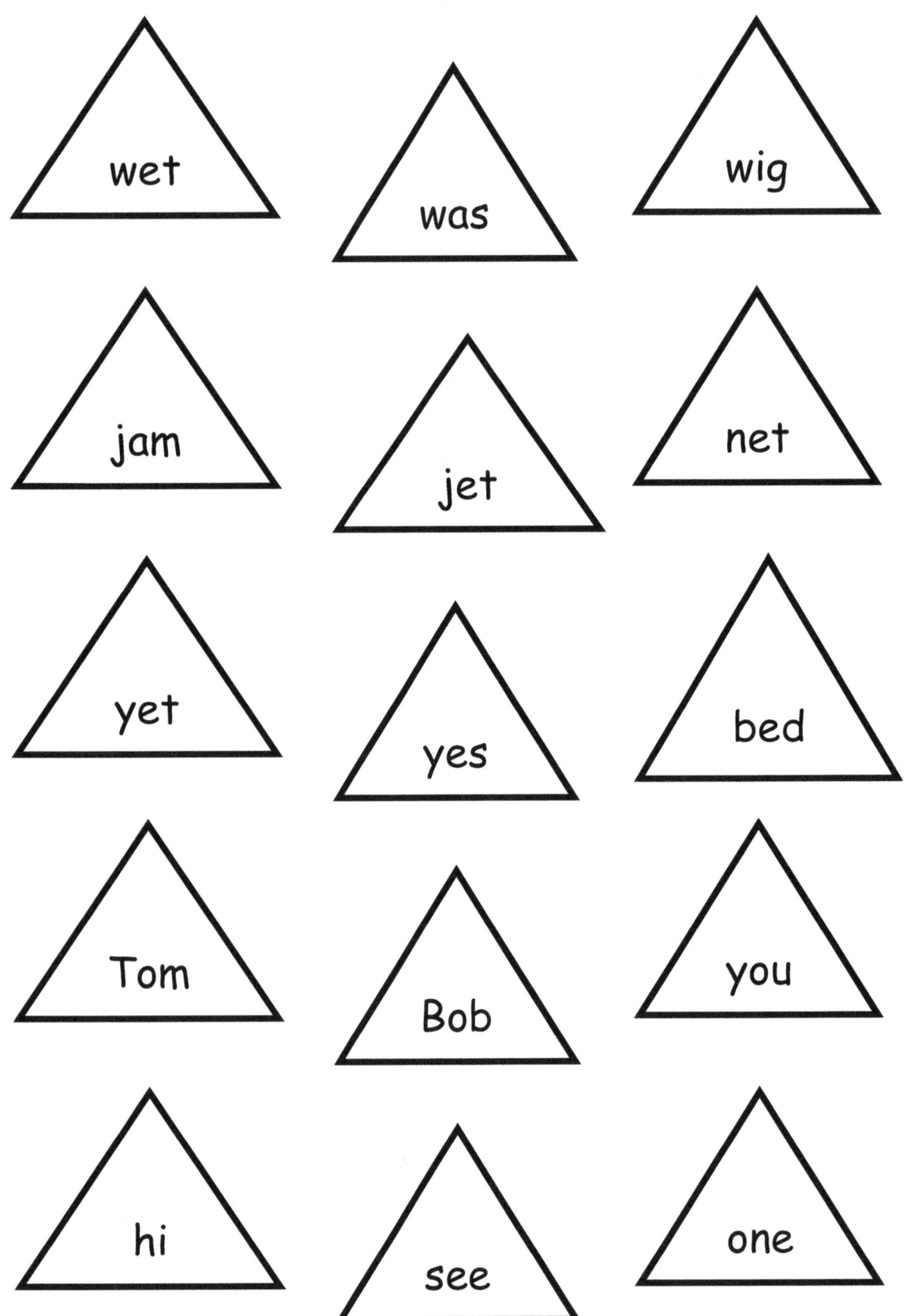

why	shy	Sam
yes	yet	you
got	the	hen
go	to	zoo
am	red	day

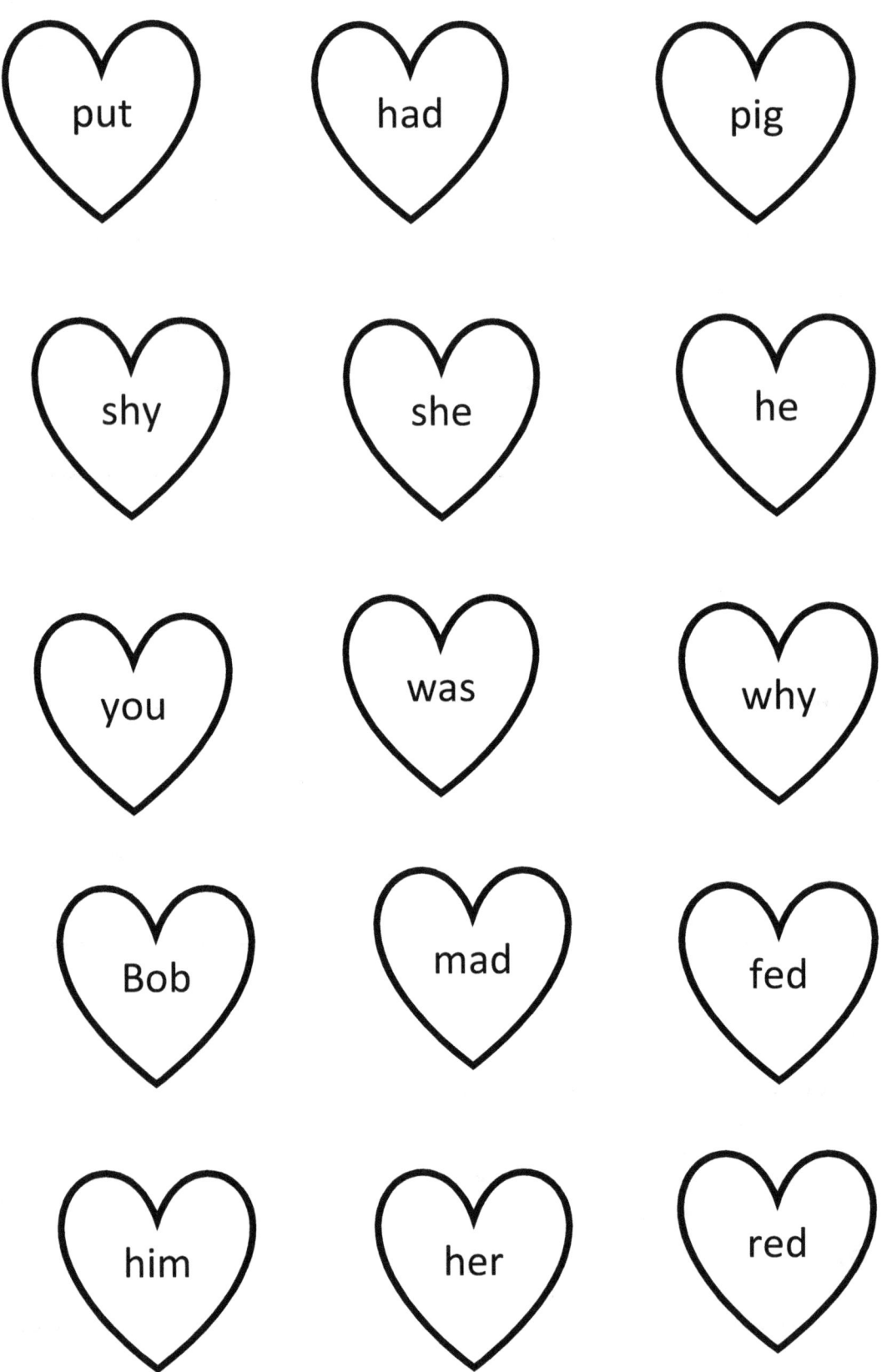

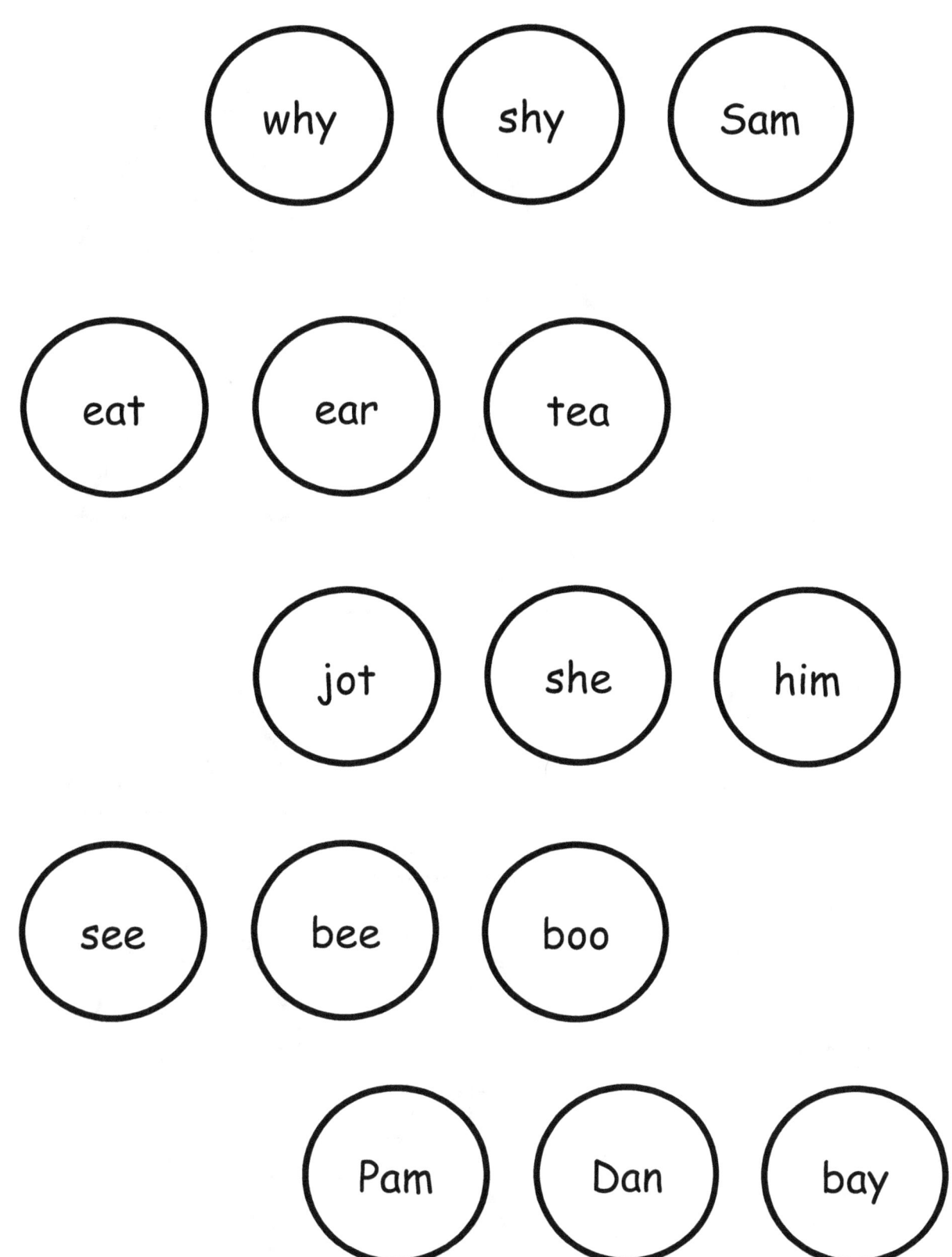

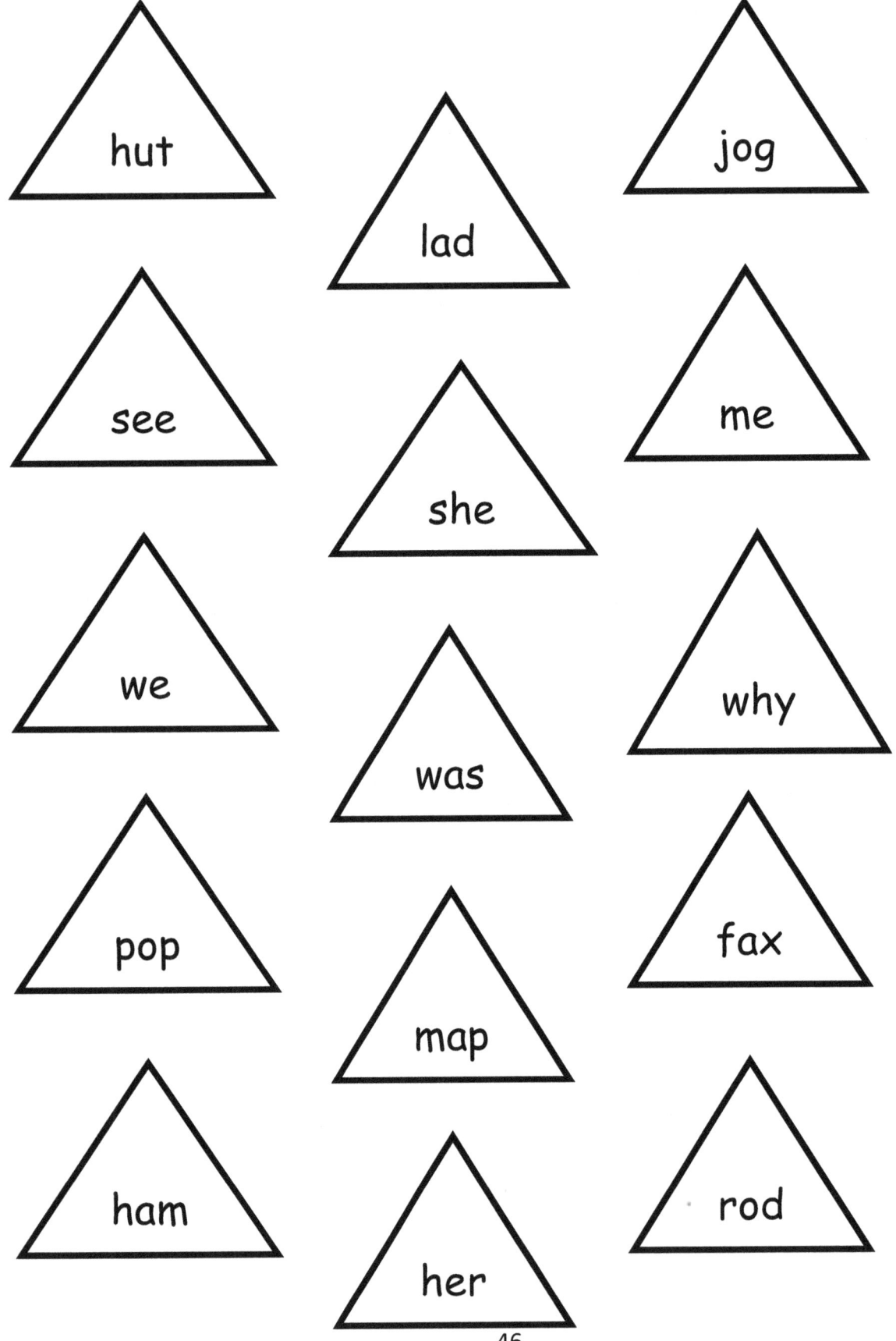

why	how	leg
eel	who	pin
our	or	of
set	bet	box
fox	dig	bed

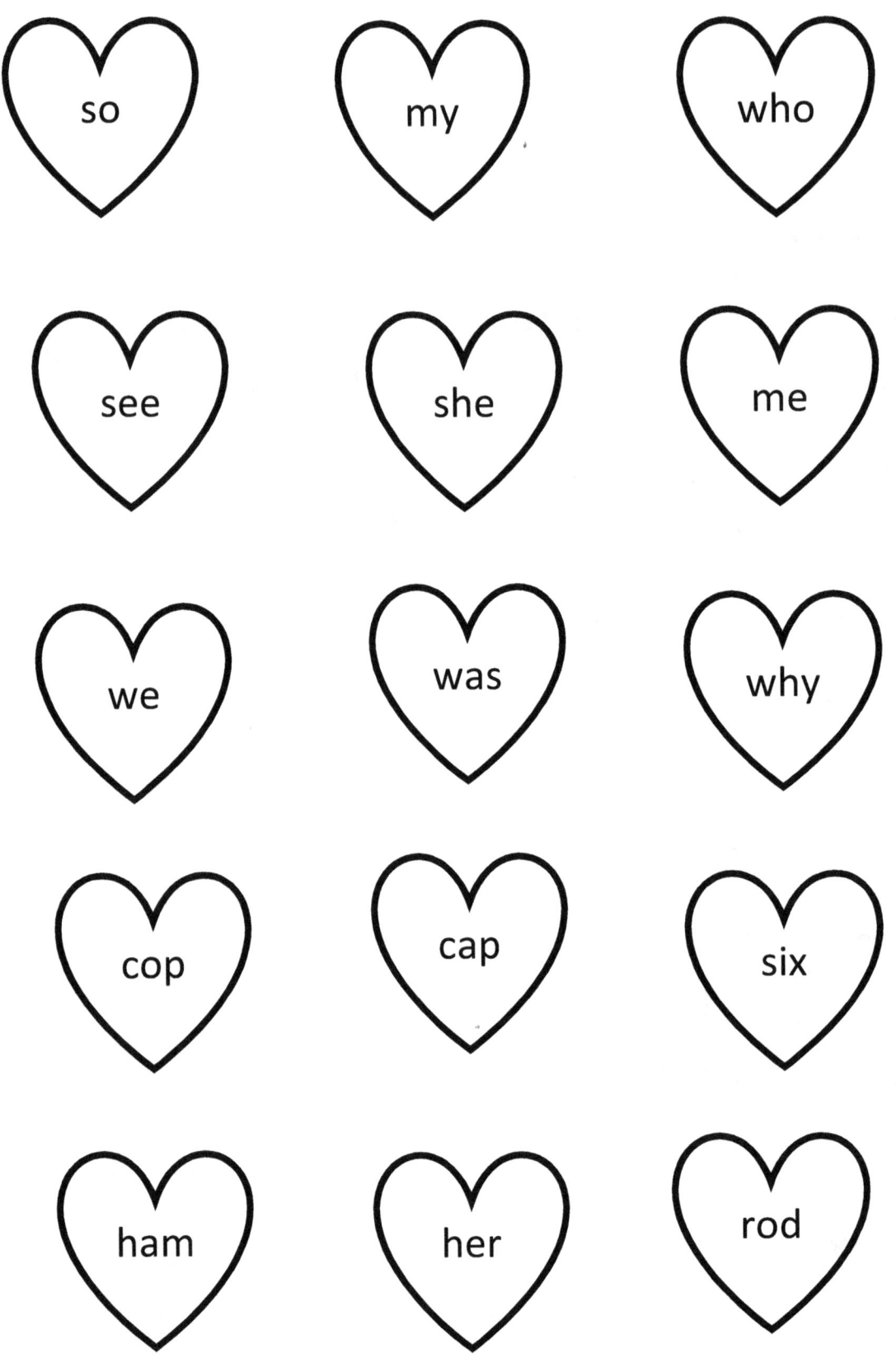

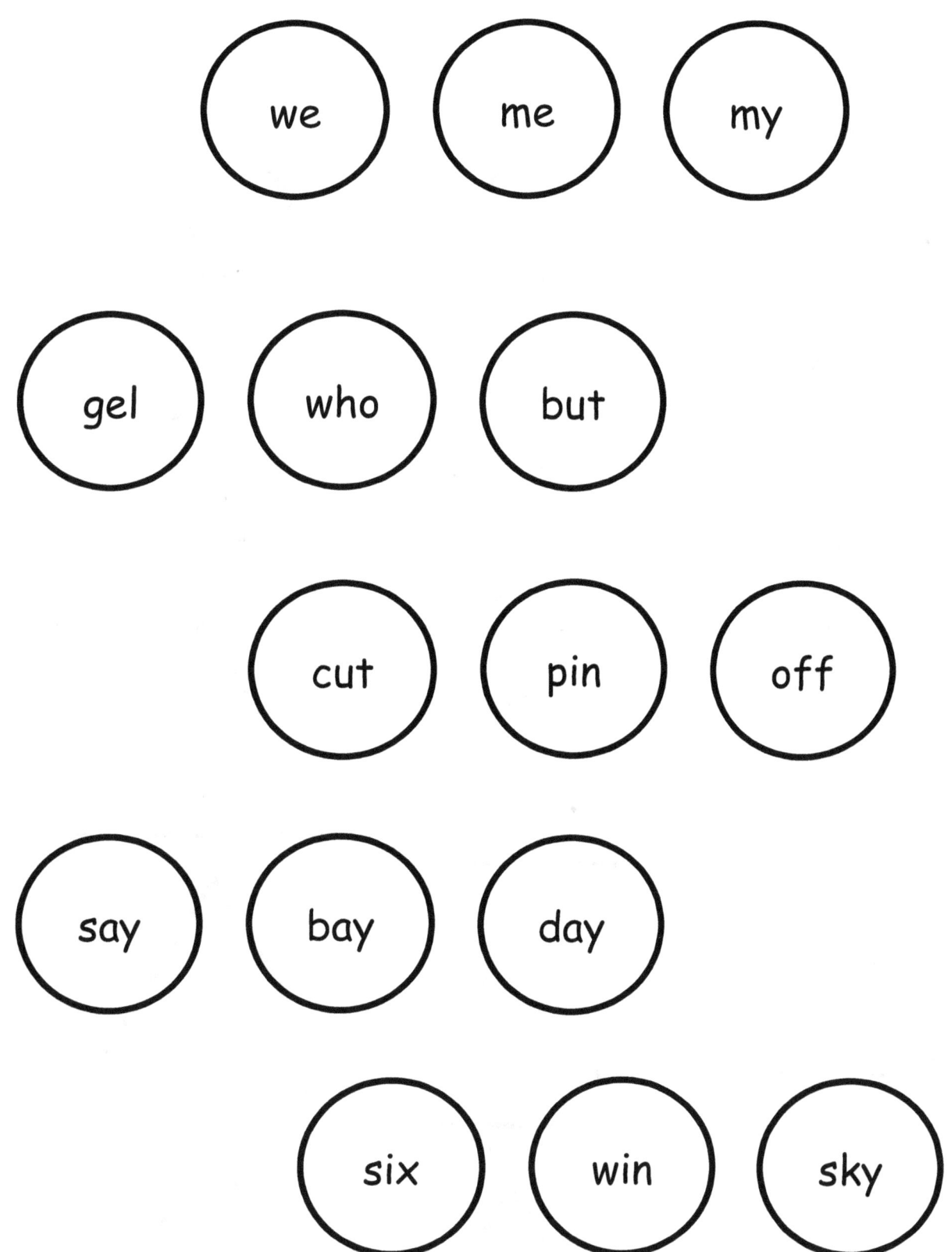

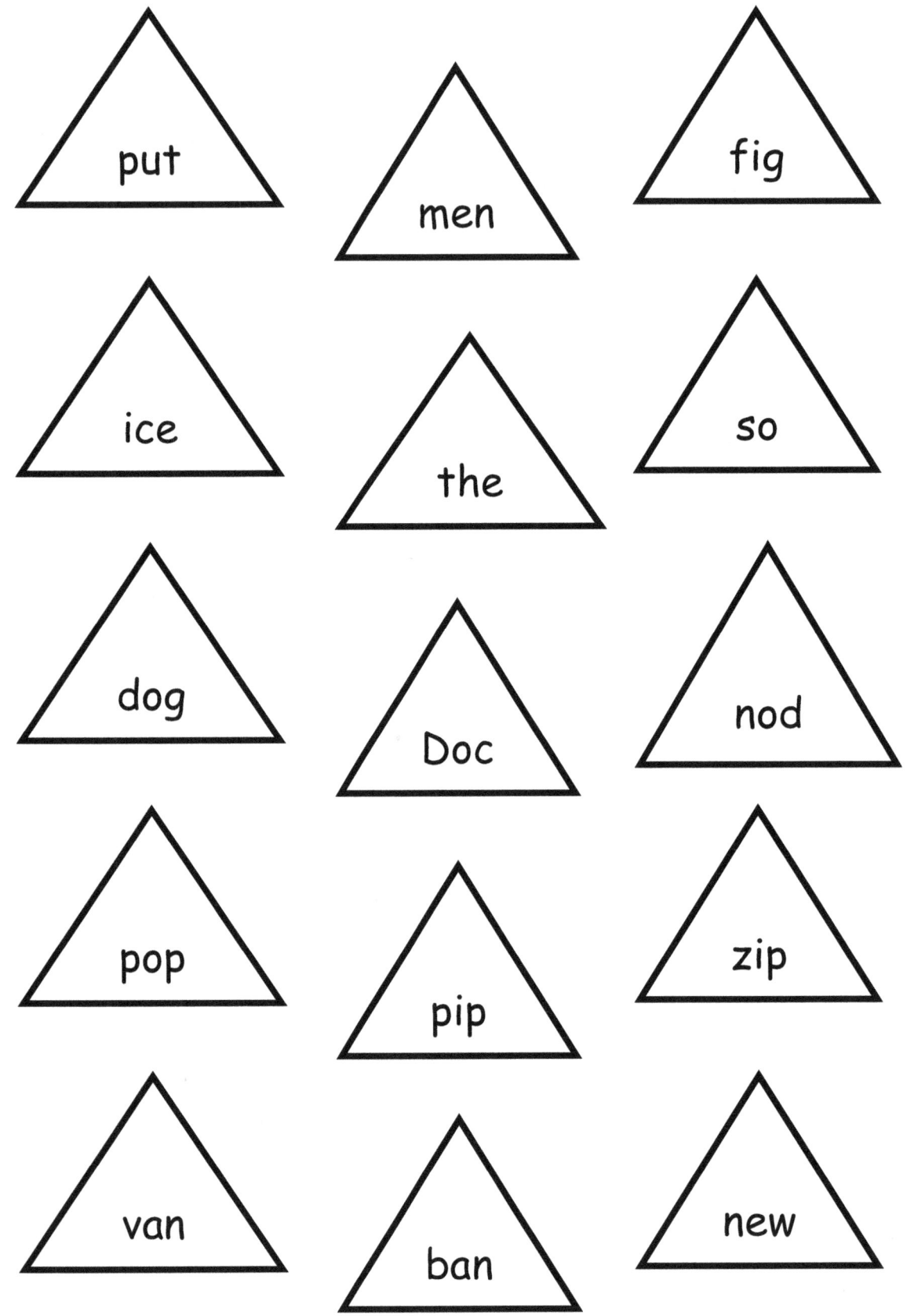

why	ate	my
gel	new	pin
how	now	wow
bow	at	day
sip	lip	dip

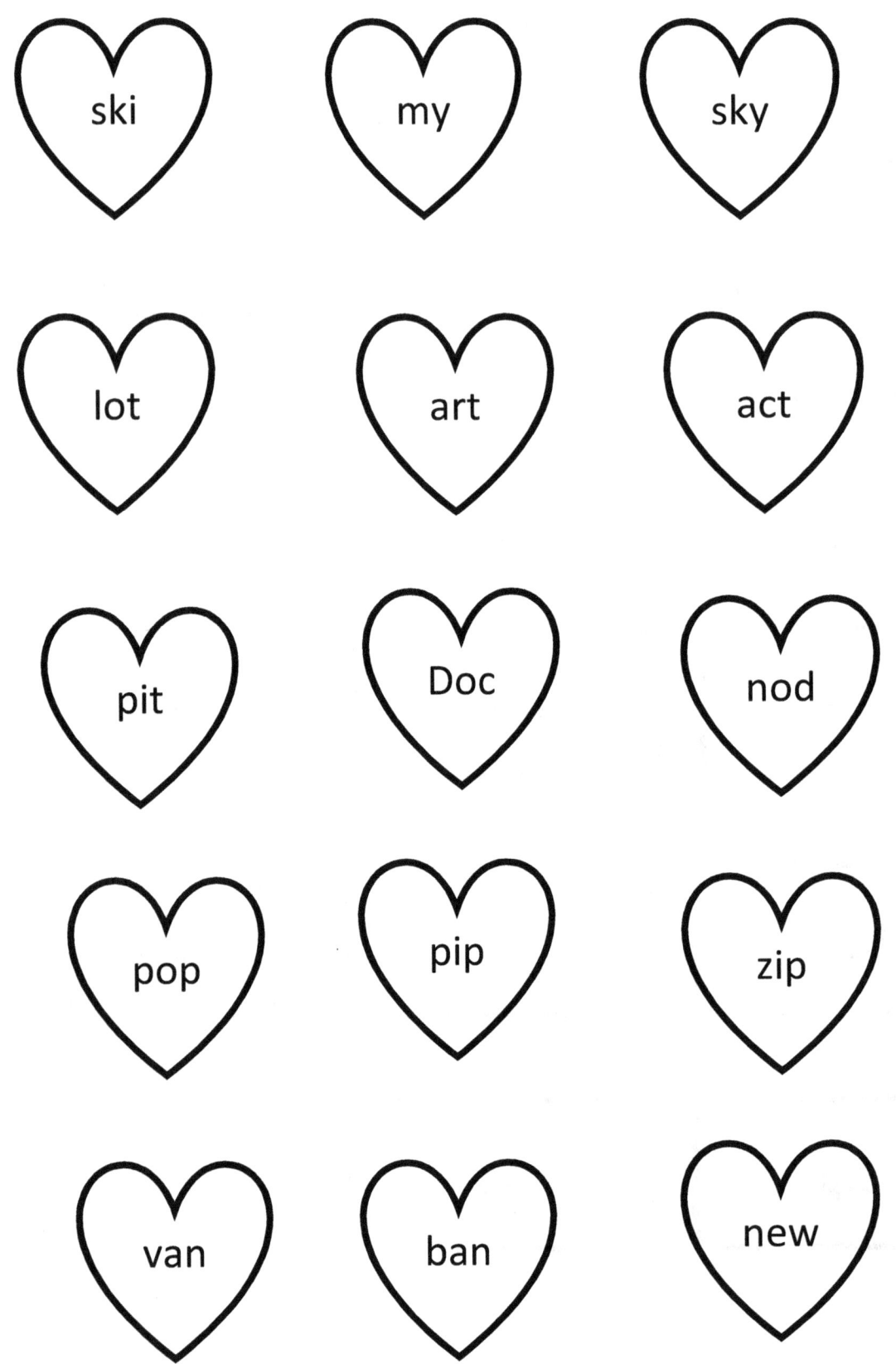

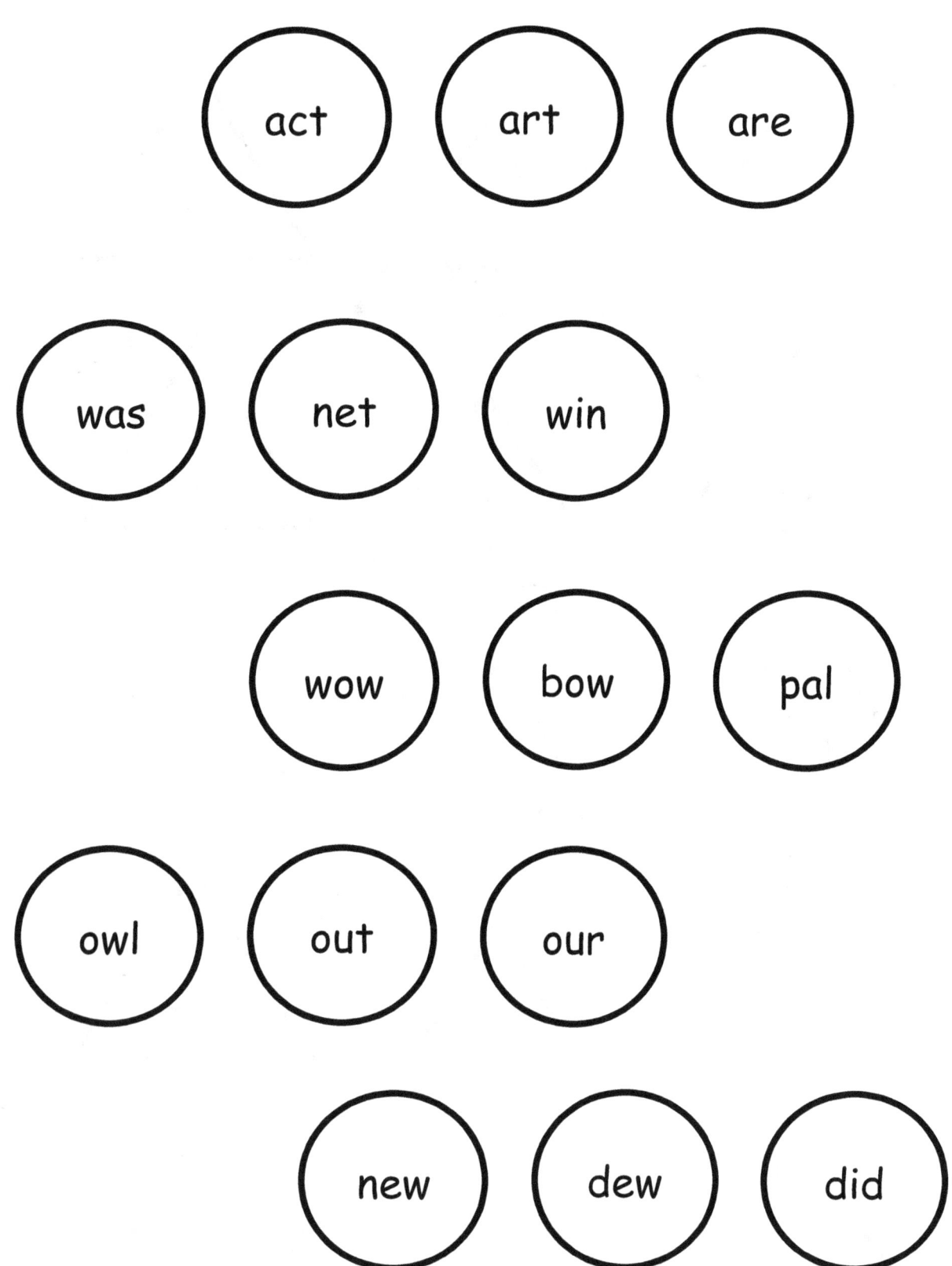

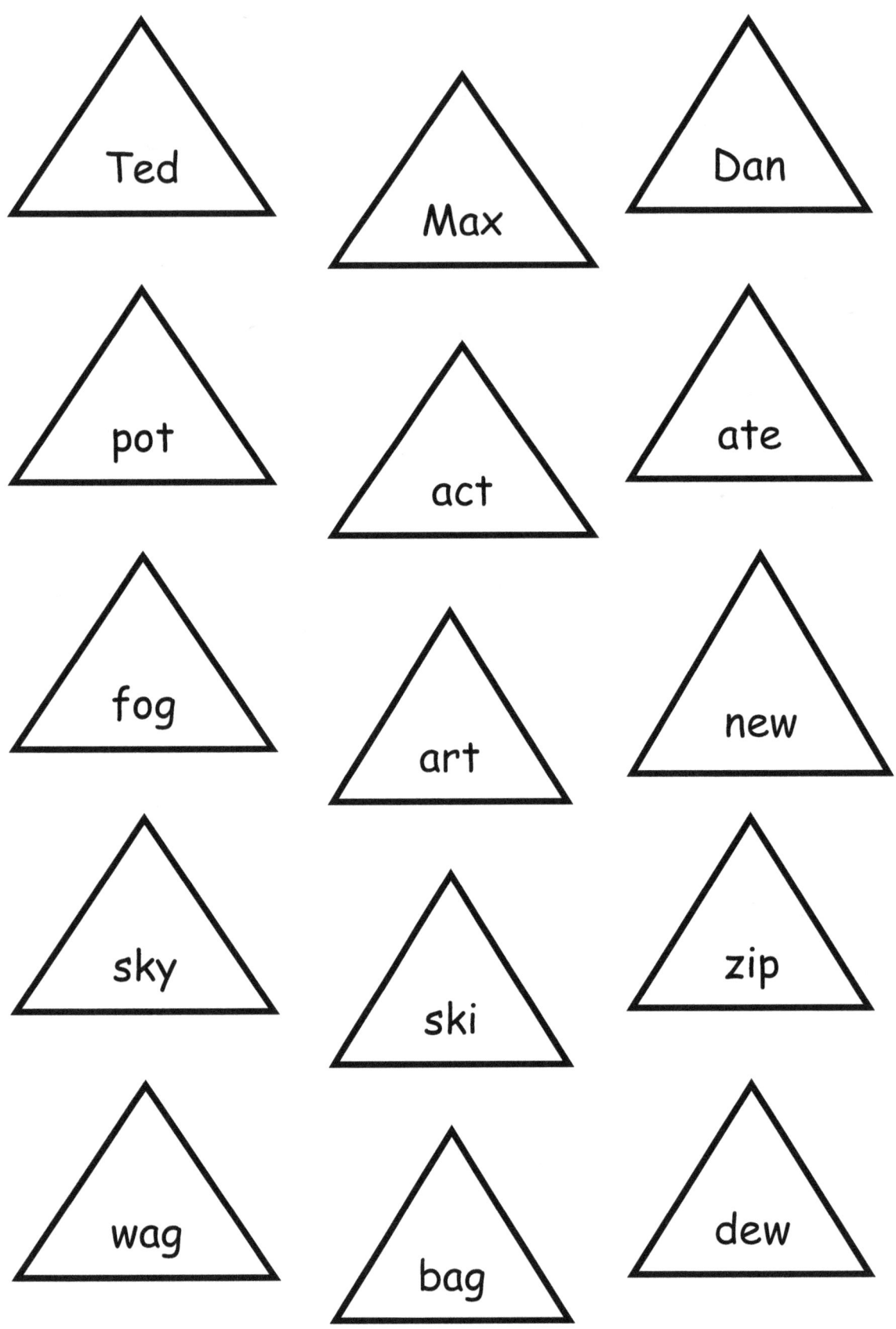

art	are	far
gas	ram	log
won	zap	lag
out	owl	you
rug	lug	dad

Write words that you like below:

Short stories

Ted got off the bus.

Ted sat on the bed.

He had a big mug of tea.

His cat sat on his lap too.

My mom had a jar of jam.

I ate all the jam.

She was not mad at me.

She was not sad too.

She got a new jar of jam

for me.

Mom and Dad got a new pot in a box.

Our dog saw the pot.

Our cat saw the box.

Mom fed our dog.

Dad fed our cat.

Our dog ate and sat on the mat.

Our cat ate and sat in the box.

He is a boy.

He is sad.

Why is he sad?

He has no toy.

But I had a toy.

"I got a car for you," I say.

The boy is not sad now.

Yay!

I ran up to my mom.

Dad and I had got a new

fan for her.

She can use it a lot.

It is so hot now.

My cat is in a box.

My dog saw her in the box.

Dog: "Why are you in the box?"

Cat: "It is my new bed now."

Dog: "I see. Can I sit in it too?"

Cat: "Yes, if you can fit."

Dog: "Oh no! I do not fit!"

YAY! You did it! Let us color the pics!

All books in this series

Book 1

Up to 3 letter words
Preschoolers, PreK and Kindergarteners
Ages 4-6

Book 2

4+ letter words
PreK, Kindergarteners and 1st graders
Ages 5-7

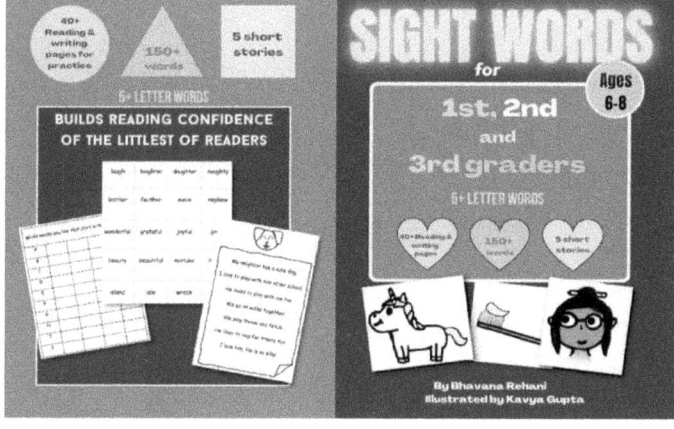

Book 3

5+ letter words
1st, 2nd and 3rd graders
Ages 6-8

www.ingramcontent.com/pod-product-compliance
Lightning Source LLC
Chambersburg PA
CBHW080942040426
42444CB00015B/3421